A Truth Universally Acknowledged

A Truth Universally Acknowledged

40 Days with Jane Austen

Rachel Mann

CANTERBURY
PRESS
Norwich

© Rachel Mann 2023

Published in 2023 by Canterbury Press
Editorial office
3rd Floor, Invicta House,
108–114 Golden Lane,
London EC1Y 0TG, UK

www.canterburypress.co.uk

Canterbury Press is an imprint of Hymns Ancient & Modern Ltd
(a registered charity)

Hymns Ancient & Modern® is a registered trademark of
Hymns Ancient & Modern Ltd
13A Hellesdon Park Road, Norwich,
Norfolk NR6 5DR, UK

Scripture quotations are from New Revised Standard Version
Bible: Anglicized Edition, copyright 1989, 1995 National
Council of the Churches of Christ in the United States of America.
Used by permission. All rights reserved worldwide.

British Library Cataloguing in Publication data

A catalogue record for this book is available
from the British Library

978-1-78622-503-0

Typeset by Regent Typesetting
Printed and bound by
CPI Group (UK) Ltd

Contents

Dedicated to those who teach, and those who persevere for the sake of love.

Introduction

It is a truth universally acknowledged...

I first met Jane Austen in September 1986. I'm ashamed to admit I didn't much like her. That initial meeting happened in the first term of Lower Sixth. Despite dire warnings from one of my science teachers that I'd be throwing away my life prospects, I'd decided to take English Literature A Level and among the first books we read was Austen's *Emma*.

Given that this Lent book centres on the novels of Jane Austen, and is, therefore, predicated on more than a passing interest in her work, it might come as a surprise to read that initially I wasn't a fan. Indeed, 50 pages into *Emma* I was ready to give up. As far as my arrogant teenaged self could see, Austen's writing was lightweight. She was only interested in romance and in social contexts that were far outside anything I cared about. After those first 50 pages, I was convinced that Jane Austen wrote Mills and Boon stories for posh people. As a chippy working-class kid, the last thing I pretended to be interested in was posh people. Nonetheless, our literature teacher assured me that Austen's writing was often laugh-out-loud funny. All I discerned was tortured sentences and archaic words. Everything seemed to take place in a drawing-room or at a ball and what *actually* took place resolved into seemingly pointless chatter about manners and horses and how much everyone's estate was worth per year. I even began to wonder if my science teacher was right: if *Emma* was representative of the novels on the A Level syllabus, then I was surely set on the road to academic perdition. In that modern phrase: I was not going to live my best life.

It was an unpromising start to a journey that ultimately led here: a book celebrating Lizzy and Darcy, Elinor and Marianne Dashwood, Fanny Price, Anne Elliot, Catherine Morland, Emma Woodhouse and all the rest of Jane Austen's immortal cast list. It was the very worst start for someone who now believes not only that Austen's writing is in the very top tier of world literature, but is also full of riches for anyone seeking to keep a holy and hopeful Lent. Indeed, that false start to my love affair with Jane Austen makes me all the more certain that she is a wonderful Lenten companion. Unlike some Austen fans (or Janeites),[1] I had to work hard to find my way into her brilliance. This slow outworking of wonder and delight has, by turns, challenged and encouraged me. I've grown to appreciate Austen's wit and *bon mots*, as well as her insight into human nature. If Austen's social context is, in so many ways, radically different from our own (and offers a sharp critique to it too), there is a richness that speaks into our present. In a post-truth world of seeming radical division, Austen's novels, with their fascination with virtue and vice, offer potent correctives.

If nothing else, I hope this book reveals my empathy towards those who struggle to find their way into the riches of Austen. For those of us used to the simple pleasures of modern popular fiction or the contemporary stylings of modern literary masters, Austen's heavily ironized style can leave a reader cold.[2] I hope that my appreciation of the struggle that some have with her writing means that this book is written with tenderness and generosity. In so many ways, Austen is not a difficult writer; she is a subtle and nuanced one, and – if nothing else – by the

---

1 As those with a passion for Austen are known. I'm not sure if I quite count as an 'all-in' Janeite.

2 Though it is worth noting that there is a case to be made that Austen deploys the first example of the free, indirect writing style much used in contemporary fiction. This is a writing technique that uses the Third Person but is imbued with the voice/consciousness of the central character. It is a technique that can create high levels of uncertainty about the reliability of the main character's narration/self-understanding. In *Emma* – as I discovered as a teenager – the reader is repeatedly misled by the self-deception of the main character.

end of this Lenten pilgrimage, I trust you will have a deeper appreciation of Austen's riches.

Is Austen appropriate for a Lenten pilgrimage? Along with Advent, Lent is one of two Christian seasons of fasting, preparation and reflection. Many of us who live in privileged nations like the UK have become accustomed to abundance. If the shifting realities of geo-politics and neo-liberal economics are resetting such notions,[3] our understanding of fasting has been refracted through notions of giving up 'sinful' (often meaning 'calorie-rich') tokens of our abundance for a few weeks; fasting becomes giving up chocolate, alcohol, fried food and the like. Certainly, there can be huge value in all of this, although my Muslim friends' commitments during Ramadan can leave me feeling as if Christian Lenten practices lack weight. If we have lost something in our modern approaches to Lent it lies, perhaps, in how far its religious, communal horizons have receded. Lent is a time when the Christian community is invited to interrogate what is left of the Body of Christ and oneself when the goods of this world are stripped away. In a seemingly post-Christian world, the horizon of penitence has narrowed. I sense that even within church communities, Lent as a time of sorrow for sin in preparation for God's sacrificial abundance – the Easter event – has been lost. There is a weightiness about Lent that is not readily recoverable. Nor, I suspect, would many wish to do so.

Nonetheless, insofar as Lent remains a potent and sober season for self- and community-examination, you might raise an eyebrow at the suggestion that Jane Austen's sparkling comedies of manners are weighty enough to speak into it. They are surely a little too frothy or happy to be suitable fodder for Lenten study, not least when, as Isaiah 58 reminds us, a time of fasting is also an invitation into the call for justice, mercy and action. For those who like a serious Lent, full of wrestling with the unstable and tortured nature of the human heart, wouldn't the writings of Graham Greene or Flannery O'Connor offer better source

---

3 Many in the UK are now hungry and live in very poor housing. There are people who are forced to practise involuntary fasting due to a lack of money.

material? Using Austen's happy romances as a Lenten study would be like someone seeking to keep a simple, holy Lent while indulging their inner George Wickham or Lydia Bennet.

That's one reading. I hope, rather, that this book reminds you of Austen's seriousness and moral purpose. I also want this book to bring cheer and some laughter. I've never considered laughter and joy to be anathema to Lent. Penitence is predicated on God's abundant delight and love, and in grim times to dwell indulgently on grimness strikes me as a token of excessive self-regard. However, I also hope that you will discover that in the midst of Austen's seemingly relentless pursuit of the 'marriage plot' there is grit and insight. As much as she has been stereotyped as a writer centred on the village and the pastoral, her novels, as often as not, unfold in cities like London and Bath; war and social change are never far from the surface. *Mansfield Park* is as much a critique of slavery as it is a tale of a country house and her characters challenge our assumptions about virtue and vice. Take Fanny Price: those readers who are established Janeites will be only too aware that Fanny has rarely been a fan favourite. She has been read as priggish or simply too dull. She lacks the spark and intelligence of a Lizzy Bennet or Elinor Dashwood. However, as I hope will emerge, the maturity and steadfastness of Fanny challenges much of what passes as virtue in the present age. Her seemingly small world exposes the flimsiness of our seemingly great one.

One of the things I hope, therefore, is that a pilgrim who uses this book will discover the 'otherness' of Austen. I don't say this to be clever. I say this to remind us that if the social milieu of Austen bears many connections and intersections with our own times – sufficiently so that she can be constantly reinterpreted for new generations – her world is not ours. The prevailing class, gender, power and religious distinctions of her world often challenge ours. Austen lived in a time when rising middle-class consumerism was held in tension with established and ancient bonds of fellowship and social obligation. We might imagine Austen's world as a happy, settled rural stasis: the High Tory world of the rich man in his castle (or country house), the poor man in his cottage, and happy concord betwixt them. However, this was, as much as ours, a time of social, cultural and political anxiety. If it is mostly hidden, war rages around the edges of Austen's world (the Napoleonic as well as the 1812 American War); Britain is a superpower on the rise towards the zenith of empire and money. Wealth flows into England from plantations still powered by slavery; status is marked by often imperceptible gradations of position, relationship and history.

For all the seeming surety of country estates 'that afford a fair prospect', there is, then, real fear: fear of falling out of the carefully stratified realms of gentility and respectability. As Jo Baker's novel *Longbourn* reveals, there are ever-present 'others' lurking in the background of the calm drawing-rooms and Assembly Room balls.[4] Sometimes, these are servants; sometimes, in *Mansfield Park*, these are slaves labouring on a distant plantation. A careful reader of Austen will be alert to aspects of her culture which may be concealed from us. For example, we might picture Regency Bath – where scenes in both *Persuasion* and *Northanger Abbey* play out – as merely an elegant place in which a plot unfolds. However, Bath also represents for Austen a kind of risky and questionable modernity – a place where identities and social position are in flux as new and old money, town and country, interact in fresh ways. A modern reader might read Bath as a symbol of elegant stasis and beauty; in Austen's time it was every bit as much in transition as Manchester in the 1830s or London in the 1960s.

As the scholar Alison Milbank notes, 'There is something really quite strange in the way that Austen is now an internationally acclaimed writer and guide to life in an age which shares none of her values.'[5] There's truth in this. However, that's the thing about Austen: she is reinvented by her devotees in each generation. Some of those adaptations may be absurd.

---

4 A version of *Pride and Prejudice* told from the servants' perspective.

5 See Alison Milbank, 'Excellent Women – Jane Austen's Afterlife: Art, Culture and Women', Westminster Abbey lecture 2018, https://audioboom.com/posts/6889254-excellent-women-jane-austen-s-afterlife-art-culture-and-religion (accessed 12.02.2023).

The recent Netflix adaptation of *Persuasion* is crap, in my view. The way it turns Anne Eliot into a sassy modern woman in an empire-line frock is an affront. However, there is a sense in which Austen is in our hands now. She cannot set the terms of her reading, or at least of her adaptation. We are not an imperial nation; we do not have obviously rigid distinctions between the classes; propriety and purity are not privileged. Inevitably, readings will be made which appropriate Austen for a post-modern world. This book, alert as it is to shifting cultural contexts, will seek to honour the facts of our present cultural realities; at the same time I am inclined to resist the temptation to turn Austen's words into *bon mots* or Insta-wisdom. I recognize how much of a challenge I face. To parcel up Austen's writings for 40 days of Lent inevitably requires an eye for the clever line or the easily packaged wisdom. The practicalities of this book required more than a little bit of parcelling up.

Not least among the reasons why Austen appeals as a Lenten focus is the ordinariness of her relationship with faith and religion. A health warning, though: Austen's Church of England is rather different to its modern equivalent. Her religion could not be further from New Wine Pentecostalism or – dare I say it – even the intemperate obsessions with the parish shown by those who have understandable concerns about the priorities of the contemporary church. The writer Paula Hollingsworth says, '[Austen] writes of clergy in her novels with great ease because she mixed naturally with them from her earliest days, and she knew and instinctively understood the world of a village rector and the role of the church in a village community.'[6] Austen's father was a village parson, as later was her brother James. Hollingsworth summarizes Austen's position on the expectations of the rural C of E in Austen's time: 'a Christian faith … was practised without excess of showy religious devotion, respected people's consciences rather than being overly intrusive, upheld the structures of society, and expected that people

---

6 Paula Hollingsworth, *The Spirituality of Jane Austen* (Oxford: Lion Books, 2017), p. 28.

would recognise their moral duty to their neighbours in a way that was appropriate to their place in society'.[7]

There is then a modesty in Austen's treatment of religion. In the case of Mr Collins, faith is shown at its most unctuous and absurd; in the case of Mr Elton, its most pretentious and overweening; in the case of Edmund Bertram, its most ordinary. Despite Austen's gentle satire of clergymen, there is none of Trollope's savagery. The cleric is part of the everyday and can be good or bad, self-serving or kind. As we travel together with Austen through Lent, I will inevitably treat with some of her 'takes' on clergy and on faith and religion. I hope to do so in a way that honours Austen; that is, I want to assume that religion and faith are not things that need to be argued for; they are part of the warp and weft. I acknowledge that, in our time, religion does not hold such a position. This book is written with generosity in mind: like Austen, I have no interest in finding a window into people's souls. Equally, I no more write with an expectation that a person who uses this book is gripped by the kind of 'religious enthusiasm' with which Austen was familiar in the shape of the Evangelical/Clapham Sect renewal movement. I want to provide space for those of much faith or little, of faith or of none, to walk deeper into this remarkable and astringent season.

The title of this volume is lifted, of course, from the opening line of Austen's most famous and most widely cherished novel, *Pride and Prejudice*. I don't mind admitting that, of all Austen's novels, this is the one I've returned to most often. It is one of my comfort reads. I can never quite get enough of Lizzy Bennet, Mr Darcy and the rest. I should add that, for all the pleasures *Pride and Prejudice* holds, I don't think it is Austen's most mature or technically sophisticated work. The later works – which focus less on characters who need to grow through an imbalance in, or lack of, virtue – are astonishingly subtle. I guess, if pushed, I'd settle on *Persuasion* as Austen's finest work. It is a remarkable piece of writing. Nonetheless, there is – not least because of the timeless 1995 BBC adaptation – something unavoidable

---

7 Hollingsworth, *The Spirituality of Jane Austen*, p. 32.

about *Pride and Prejudice*. I could have written this entire book based on quotes from it. At one point I was tempted so to do. However, ultimately there is simply too much good stuff across the six completed novels.

Jane Austen had a rarely matched insight into human character and our abiding human problems. This provides a lively and spirited accompaniment to the rigours and promises of Lent; rather like the season of Lent itself, Austen exposes human frailty, caprice and pomposity while ultimately inviting us into hopeful and joyous visions of human relationships and society. In the midst of familiar passages, I hope there are moments of surprise and unexpected challenges. I trust that, along the way, you will come to appreciate how Austen can faithfully be read as a feminist as well as a critic of slavery. I trust also that she will lead us, as readers, deeper into an appreciation of the absurdities as well as the glories of being human. I hope that across these 40 days we will see in her writings a demanding genius, as well as a creativity that challenges us to treat more honestly with both ourselves and the living God.

In writing this book, I am especially grateful for the comments of Rachel Blanchflower and Mads Davies, whose careful attention to the draft manuscript, often under the most trying personal circumstances, have improved this book immeasurably. If there are errors in the readings of Austen on offer in this book, they are all mine!

How to read this book

My primary piece of advice is simple: remember, this is your book. It is entirely up to you how you read it. Please use and meditate on its contents as you see fit. I am delighted that you have a copy and I want you to find a way through it that enriches you. If, after setting out hopefully, you find after a couple of days that the book is a bit 'meh', I hope you'll keep going. However, if you need to throw it to the floor in disappointment, that's OK too. It's your book.

While it is structured with the 40 days of Lent in mind, I hope the book may offer encouragement, challenge and inspiration at any time of the year. Equally, while it is not written as a 'group study' book, I can readily see how it might be used by a home group or an online study group. Please adapt as you see fit. Sometimes readers get in touch to ask my permission to adapt a reflection or meditation from one of my books. Provided you're not going to be using the material for nefarious purposes, please just crack on. Enjoy, reflect, pray and dream as you feel drawn.

Having said all of the above, I have, of course, given considerable time and energy to the composition of this book. So a note about the structural decisions I've made. Tempting though it was to simply give over a week of Lent to each one of Austen's six completed novels, I have resisted. Rather, I've grouped the readings according to book, hopefully to help the reader feel they are reading consistently without too much jumping around. I've deliberately granted more days to two books: *Pride and Prejudice* and *Persuasion*. I start my book with the former, despite the fact that it was the second of Austen's novels to be published. I begin this way because I want to acknowledge it as Austen's best-known novel. For those who aren't Austen geeks, it will offer an accessible way into this Lent book. As for *Persuasion*, as it is my current favourite Austen novel, I couldn't resist offering up a few extra days on it. The sharp-eyed will also note one further imbalance: I grant seven days to *Sense and Sensibility* and a mere five to *Northanger Abbey*. I had not planned this! I felt I had to give an extra date to the former in order to give a non-Austen fan a better feel for the shape of the novel. If only Lent were longer. The meditation on *Northanger Abbey* I was forced to leave out was a banger.

The fact is that 365 days would be insufficient to capture the brilliance of Austen; allowing myself only 40 is nigh on impossible. If it is self-indulgent to give more space to one or two of the novels, then so be it. I do not, in this selection, claim any sort of objectivity. I am led by personal passion and, I hope, more than a smidgeon of the Spirit's wild energy. Please don't shout at me or shake your fist at the heavens if, when you've completed this book, one of your favourite passages has been omitted. Let the absence be a spur to you to go off and look again at the novel in question and make your own response as you feel drawn. I beg your indulgence: very many of the passages I write about reflect sections of the novel that bring happiness to me. That decision has made writing this book a pleasure; I hope my pleasure communicates itself to you.

Should you read or reread Austen's novels before starting this Lent book? It would be remiss of me to dissuade you from reading Jane Austen. If you've not read any Austen at all, please do take a closer look. If you've not read Austen for a while, there are always fresh wonders to be found. However, I don't want anyone to add another potentially guilt-inducing thing to their 'to-do' list. If you've got this far, then you've already made a commitment. Please don't add to your stress. Whether you are a relative Austen newbie or an old hand, I've included a short summary of each novel by way of orientation and *aide-memoire*. There are other more substantial 'blow-by-blow' summaries available online.

Equally, you might find that one of the many admirable TV and film adaptations provides the simplest way to jog your memory about the shape of Austen's novels. Please be warned, however: not all adaptations are equal and all adaptations make editorial decisions. The 2007 adaptation of *Mansfield Park*, starring Billie Piper, may have many fine points, but its representation of Fanny as a girl with sass is unfaithful to the original text. If memory serves, it is that adaptation which includes the fabulous line, 'Run mad as often as you choose, but do not faint.' It is a great line, but it is taken from one of Austen's pieces of juvenilia. Equally, much as everyone loves Colin Firth's damp shirt as he emerges from Pemberley's pond in the 1995 adaptation of *Pride and Prejudice*, it's not part of Austen's book. Be warned! The Jane Austen industry rather does like to turn her work into part of the burgeoning Regency Romance boom.[8]

---

8 There are also audio drama versions of Austen's works. The podcast industry, too, provides fertile ground for the Austen obsessive. In terms of the best adaptations of Austen, I have views: the 1995 BBC *Pride and*

I hope, for each day of Lent, you will find time to read the set passage and meditation. They offer, I believe, a space to pause and reflect, and both invite self-examination and provide an opportunity to reflect hopefully on God and this troublous world of which we are part. Jane Austen wrote a small number of surviving prayers. I use sections of them to punctuate this Lenten pilgrimage of hope and repentance.[9]

Prejudice is definitive. Equally, the 1995 film of *Sense and Sensibility* is beyond wonderful and adapts the novel in an imaginative but faithful way. Honourable mentions should be given to both the 1996 and 2020 versions of *Emma*. I think the 2007 BBC *Persuasion* is very watchable, and the 1995 version is classic. 2007 was a solid year for Austen, with adaptations of both *Northanger Abbey* and *Mansfield Park*.

9 The positioning of the prayers assumes that you begin on Ash Wednesday and then take each Sunday off. The full text of Austen's three surviving prayers can be found online. For example, Christianity.Com, https://www.christianity.com/wiki/prayer/surviving-prayers-of-jane-austen.html (accessed 12.02.2023).

The Novels – An Overview

I've come very much to appreciate a good précis or – on a Netflix or Disney+ show – the recap. I hope these summaries (presented in order of publication) offer a fixed reference point to which you can return as you need. If you become disorientated by my selection you can always return here for a 'Previously on ...' refresher moment. Acknowledging that some of Austen's novels are less well known than others, some of these summaries are more substantial than others.

Sense and Sensibility (1811)

Austen's debut novel focuses on the shifting fortunes of the Dashwood sisters, Elinor and Marianne. At the beginning of the novel they live with their mother and much younger sister, Margaret, at Norland Park. Their father has just died and the Park has been inherited by their older stepbrother John and his wife Fanny. The Dashwoods have to leave and move to Barton Cottage in Devon, on the estate of Sir John Middleton, a distant relative. Both sisters fall in love: Elinor with Edward Ferrers, Fanny Dashwood's brother, and Marianne with John Willoughby, a dashing country gentleman. They both face the loss of their love interest. Despite the apparent closeness of Willoughby and Marianne, one day he suddenly leaves Devon, to be seen next in London engaged to another woman. Marianne is devastated and, ultimately, falls ill. When the caddish truth behind Willoughby's actions is revealed, Marianne finally comes to realize that she could not be happy with him and recognizes that she can be happy with the older, more stolid Colonel Brandon. Elinor herself faces trials as she discovers that the man she loves (and whom she believes loves her), Edward Ferrars, is secretly betrothed to Lucy Steele, a fortune-hunting woman. She bears this disappointment with great self-control and is prepared to let Edward go. However, when Edward is disinherited by his mother, Lucy drops him for Edward's brother. Edward, by now set on a path to become a humble clergyman, is free to seek Elinor's hand. With great joy their lives are joined together and the two sisters and their husbands live within walking distance of one another. This subtle and witty novel of secrets and suppression, lies and seduction, explores how sense and sensibility must be kept in balance and portrays a world where rigid social convention clashes with the impulses of the heart.

Pride and Prejudice (1813)

Austen's most famous novel centres on the immortal relationship between Elizabeth (Lizzy) Bennet and Fitzwilliam Darcy as they negotiate their initial mutual mistrust and dislike, their pride and prejudice, until they are both changed and can see each other clearly. The novel follows the shifting fortunes of the Bennet daughters, Jane, Elizabeth, Mary, Kitty and Lydia – genteel and respectable but with no fortune – as they seek to make their way in a world of wealthy landowners, snobbery and rakish cads, with little to recommend themselves but genteel birth. At the outset of the novel, a wealthy young man, Mr Bingley, arrives in the Bennets' neighbourhood, along with his sisters and his extremely wealthy friend Darcy. Bingley is deeply attracted to the beautiful Jane Bennet, but Darcy and Bingley's sisters are convinced that Jane's family are unworthy of him and detach Bingley from Jane.

Despite himself, and with a good deal of self-disgust, Darcy finds himself falling in love with Elizabeth. Elizabeth becomes convinced that Darcy is a cruel and aloof man, not least when she gets to know an officer in the militia, Mr Wickham, and hears that Darcy has treated him unjustly. As Darcy and Elizabeth encounter each other in a range of settings, the truth becomes clearer: while Darcy has behaved unjustly towards Jane, he has supported the naughty Mr Wickham far better than he deserves. Slowly, Darcy and Elizabeth begin to see each other clearly and their prejudices fall away as love blossoms. However, all seems lost when Wickham runs off with Elizabeth's youngest sister, Lydia, with no real intention of marrying her. Elizabeth is convinced that she will never see Darcy again. Darcy, however – despite his contempt for Wickham – lays out a huge sum to induce Wickham to marry Lydia. Finally, Bingley and Jane are reconciled; Lizzy and Darcy too are able to marry. *Pride and Prejudice* is a story about love, but it is also a novel about the search for happiness and self-knowledge in a world of strict social rules, where a middle-class woman must marry well to survive.

Mansfield Park (1814)

Mansfield Park tells the story of Fanny Price from childhood to young adulthood. As a child Fanny is sent to live with her aunt and uncle, Sir Thomas and Lady Bertram, at Mansfield Park. Fanny grows up with her four cousins: Tom, Edmund, Maria and Julia. She feels awkward because of her lack of proper manners and exposure to luxury and wealth. She is homesick and especially misses her brother William. In Fanny's early years at Mansfield her relations generally neglect her. Only her cousin Edmund goes out of his way to make Fanny feel comfortable, establishing an intense bond between them.

As Fanny grows up she serves as a companion to Lady Bertram. Sir Thomas leaves with Tom for business in Antigua. Maria begins a courtship with the rich but stupid Mr Rushworth. Rushworth and Maria agree to marry, on the condition that they wait to wed until Sir Thomas returns from the West Indies. That summer, siblings Mary and Henry Crawford come to stay with the Grants at the rectory near Mansfield Park.

Both of them are attractive and charming and they quickly befriend the Bertrams. Tom returns from the West Indies, with Sir Thomas to follow in the late autumn. Henry flirts with both Julia and Maria, despite Maria's engagement. Meanwhile, Mary and Edmund become emotionally close. This upsets Fanny, who, over the years, has fallen in love with Edmund.

The young people decide to put on a play. Edmund and Fanny resist, though eventually Edmund joins in. Fanny, however, holds out. Sir Thomas returns from Antigua just before the play is ready. He is angry, thinking the theatricals are totally improper, and puts an end to the fun. Maria, who had hoped Henry would ask to marry her, gives up her dreams and marries Mr Rushworth. Mary becomes friends with Fanny and Henry decides that, as a game, he will try to seduce Fanny. Fanny, meanwhile, is caught in the middle of Mary and Edmund's romance, which is a constant source of pain. Edmund tries to determine if Mary would marry him, but Mary is unwilling to commit because Edmund is a younger son, fortune-less, and a clergyman.

Fanny's sailor brother William visits Mansfield Park and Sir Thomas, who has warmed to Fanny since his return from Antigua, throws a formal ball in her honour. Henry has accidentally fallen in love with her while trying to seduce her. He leaves for London, where he secures a promotion for William in an attempt to win Fanny's heart. He then proposes to Fanny, who rejects him, much to Sir Thomas's disapproval. Fanny returns to her childhood home in Portsmouth for the first time in many years. Fanny loathes the chaos she finds in Portsmouth, but becomes close to her younger sister, Susan. Henry visits Fanny at Portsmouth and reiterates his affection for her. Fanny begins to warm to him, and Mary encourages her to marry him. Soon afterwards, however, Fanny receives word that Tom is gravely ill. She worries and longs to return to Mansfield. Then Fanny hears rumours that Henry and Maria have run away together. In a letter, Edmund confirms the rumours and adds the news that Julia and Mr Yates, a friend of Tom's, have eloped. Fanny returns home to Mansfield and brings her sister Susan with her.

THE NOVELS - AN OVERVIEW

When Edmund talks to Mary about the affair between Maria and Henry, she does not condemn their actions, but rather complains about the fact that they were found out. As a result, Edmund is disgusted and terminates his relationship with her. Henry is totally excommunicated from the Bertram household. Maria, now disgraced, leaves Mansfield to live in a house far away with her aunt Mrs Norris. Julia and Mr Yates attempt to make amends with Sir Thomas and are forgiven. Mary moves away from Mansfield, settling in London. Edmund thinks romantically about Fanny for the first time and falls in love with her. They marry and lead a happy life together. *Mansfield Park* is Austen's most complex work; a powerful portrayal of change and continuity, scandalous misdemeanours and true integrity. It touches on themes of power and slavery, as well as of persistence, constancy and virtue.

Emma (1816)

Rich, beautiful and single, Emma Woodhouse is content with her life in the village of Highbury and sees no need for either love or marriage. Nothing delights her more than interfering in the romantic lives of others. However, when she ignores the warnings of her good friend Mr Knightley and attempts to arrange a suitable match for her protégée Harriet Smith, her carefully laid plans soon unravel. Emma is convinced that her friend deserves a gentleman, though Harriet's own parentage is unknown. She coaxes Harriet into rejecting Mr Martin, a farmer whom Emma believes is below Harriet, and encourages her friend to admire Mr Elton, the local vicar. It turns out that all the signs that Emma interprets as evidence of Mr Elton's interest in Harriet were in fact intended for Emma herself. Harriet is heartbroken and Emma mortified. Humiliated by Emma's rejection of him and her attempt to pair him with Harriet, Mr Elton retires to Bath. Emma realizes that personal pride in her judgement and her desires for Harriet blinded her to the real situation. She resolves never to play matchmaker in the future.

Jane Fairfax, an accomplished and beautiful young woman, returns to Highbury to visit her aunt and grandmother, Miss Bates and Mrs Bates. Orphaned at an early age, Jane is expected to become a governess. Emma greets her arrival with mixed admiration and jealousy. Frank Churchill, the son of Mr Weston (the husband of Emma's former governess), is also due to visit after many delays. He lives with his snobbish aunt and uncle, Mr and Mrs Churchill, in London. Emma anticipates his arrival with pleasure and finds him charming. Mr Knightley, on the other hand, immediately dislikes him as superficial and silly. Frank's flattering attentions soon single out Emma. Mr Elton returns from Bath with his new bride, the self-important and ghastly Mrs Elton (whose family have made money through the Bristol slave trade), who takes a liking to Jane and a distaste to Emma.

Misperceptions abound as various characters speculate about developing romances. Emma enjoys Frank's attention but ultimately decides he is not for her. Mrs Weston suspects a match between Mr Knightley and Jane, which Emma vehemently dismisses. Mr Knightley saves Harriet from social humiliation, asking her to dance when Mr Elton snubs her. Emma encourages what she believes to be Harriet's developing interest in Frank. Everyone, except Mr Knightley, regards Frank and Emma as a match. Knightley believes Frank to be attached to Jane. Emma laughingly dismisses this, believing she knows the secrets of each character's heart. When Mr Knightley reprimands her for mocking the harmless Miss Bates, however, she feels great remorse and resolves to improve her behaviour to the Bateses. Mrs Churchill dies, setting in motion the shocking revelation that Frank and Jane have been secretly engaged. Frank's courtship of Emma was a cover to hide his true attachment, which his aunt opposed. Through a series of painful misunderstandings, Jane broke off their engagement and was about to take up a governess position. Frank frantically obtained his uncle's approval to marry her and the two are reconciled.

Emma also misperceived Harriet's interest in Frank, as Harriet reveals herself to be in love with Mr Knightley. In turn, Emma's distress over this revelation triggers her own realization that she, too, is in love with Mr Knightley. Emma is anguished over her various misperceptions about Frank, Jane, Harriet and herself. She reproves herself for being blinded by her own desires and self-interest. Emma fears that Mr Knightley will confess his love for Harriet, but to her surprise and delight, he declares his love for Emma. Emma happily accepts Mr Knightley's proposal and she later has the opportunity of reflecting with Frank that, despite their many blunders, they have both been luckier than they deserve. Emma is further cheered upon learning that Harriet has accepted a second proposal from Mr Martin. The novel concludes with three marriages: Harriet and Mr Martin, Jane and Frank, and Emma and Mr Knightley. It is, then, a great novel of social misunderstanding and youthful over-confidence, as well as class, secrets and manners.

Northanger Abbey (1818)

Northanger Abbey is the most youthful and optimistic of Jane Austen's novels, reflecting the fact that it was the first of her novels to be completed. It tells the story of young, impressionable Catherine Morland, who loves fashionable gothic romance novels, and her encounters with the sophisticated Tilneys and their family home, Northanger Abbey.

Naive and clumsy, Catherine is thrilled to be invited by family friends, Mr and Mrs Allen, to visit Bath. Catherine soon meets a witty young clergyman, Henry Tilney. When Catherine and Mrs Allen meet an old classmate of Mrs Allen's named Mrs Thorpe, Catherine becomes fast friends with Mrs Thorpe's daughter, Isabella. The Thorpes already know Catherine's older brother James, who is up at Oxford with Mrs Thorpe's son, John. Catherine and Isabella become inseparable, but Catherine continues to look for Henry Tilney, who seems to have left Bath.

Catherine discovers that Isabella and James have feelings for one another. Catherine is introduced to Isabella's brother John, who asks Catherine to dance with him at a ball. Despite thinking John ill-mannered, Catherine has too little confidence in her own judgement to decide that she does not like him. At another ball, Catherine meets Henry's sister, Eleanor. While Catherine wishes to develop an acquaintance with the Tilneys, the Thorpes get in the way. They contrive repeatedly to frustrate Catherine's emerging relationship with Henry and his sister. It is through good fortune more than planning that Catherine and the Tilneys become better acquainted.

Isabella tells Catherine that she and James are engaged, but she worries that the Morlands will not approve of her as a daughter-in-law. Catherine had not suspected their romance and is shocked and overjoyed. At the next ball, Catherine dances with Henry, while Isabella, who told Catherine that she did not intend to dance, dances with Henry's older brother Captain Frederick Tilney. The next day, when Isabella learns how much the Morlands will give her and James to set up home, she seems disappointed about the amount and suggests that Mr Morland has not been generous. Catherine feels hurt, but Isabella says she is only disappointed that she and James must wait several years to marry.

Catherine is thrilled to receive an invitation to travel to the Tilneys' home, Northanger Abbey, an old building like the ones in the books she loves to read. Isabella encourages Catherine to marry John, and Catherine is dumbfounded to hear that John wants to marry her. She tells Isabella that she is interested in Henry, not John. However, in the days before Catherine's departure for Northanger she observes a flirtation between Isabella and Frederick, with growing alarm. She asks Henry to tell his brother to leave Bath, but Henry says no outside interference should be needed to ensure Isabella's loyalty to James.

Catherine leaves Bath with the Tilneys. Catherine hopes to uncover a mystery at Northanger, as she has developed a theory that General Tilney is a villain and murdered his wife. She sneaks alone to Mrs Tilney's room, where she is discovered by Henry. Learning of her suspicions, Henry urges her to be a better judge of situations in the future. She feels humiliated and sure he will never love her now, but he is only kinder to her after this. Catherine receives a letter from James saying that his engagement to Isabella is off. He advises Catherine to leave Northanger before Frederick Tilney arrives to announce that *he* is engaged to Isabella. Soon after, the General hints that he hopes Catherine and Henry will marry. Catherine hopes that Henry feels the same way.

Soon after, the General leaves for London for a few days and Henry leaves Northanger. One night the General returns unexpectedly. He sends a distraught Eleanor to tell Catherine that she is to be unceremoniously expelled from the house the next morning. Catherine is shocked, but tries to hide this from Eleanor. A miserable Catherine returns home, where she is greeted joyfully. Her family resents the way she has been treated, but counsels that she forget about it. Catherine mopes around the house, but no one guesses that she is in love.

Finally, Henry asks Catherine to marry him. He explains that the General was misled in Bath by John to believe that Catherine was very rich, then subsequently told by John in London that she was quite poor. The General wanted Catherine to marry Henry when he believed she was an heiress, then rushed back to expel her from Northanger when he learned she was not. Henry, to his father's shock, refuses to obey the command to forget her. The Morlands give their permission for Catherine and Henry's marriage on the condition that the General give his. Eventually, after Eleanor marries a rich Viscount and the General learns that Catherine is not as poor as he had been led to believe, he gives his permission and Catherine and Henry are married. *Northanger Abbey* is a novel rich in satire about the gothic and romantic novels popular in Austen's day. However, it is also a surprisingly tender and generous story about a young woman's emerging self-understanding and capacity to discern between truth and falsehood.

Persuasion (1818)

Persuasion is a novel of second chances and missed opportunities centred on Anne Elliot, who is no longer young (she is 27!) and who has few romantic prospects. Eight years prior to the opening scenes of the novel, she was persuaded by her family to break off her engagement to poor, handsome naval officer Frederick Wentworth. Much of the novel – set primarily in fashionable Lyme Regis and Bath – centres on what happens when they meet again. It is also a satire of vanity and pretension, and a mature, tender love story tinged with heartache.

The novel opens with the vain Sir Walter Elliott, baronet of Kellynch Hall, poring over the Elliot family history. His wife died 14 years previously, leaving behind three daughters: the youngest, Mary, is married to the wealthy Charles Musgrove. Proud and beautiful Elizabeth is the eldest and her father's favourite; Anne is gentle and subdued and often overlooked. Their mother's best friend, Lady Russell, helped Sir Walter raise his children. The Elliots have fallen into debt due to Sir Walter's extravagant spending and decide to rent their estate to Admiral and Mrs Croft and move to Bath. Admiral and Mrs Croft are a respectable, well-off, well-mannered Navy couple. The arrival of Mrs Croft stirs powerful memories for Anne, as she is the sister of Captain Wentworth.

While Sir Walter, Elizabeth and Mrs Clay (Elizabeth's close friend and a widow) travel to Bath, Anne visits her sister Mary at Uppercross to help out and keep her company. The rest of the Musgrove family live nearby at the Great House. Mr and Mrs Musgrove have two grown daughters, Henrietta and Louisa. Captain Wentworth arrives to visit his sister, Mrs Croft, and quickly becomes a favourite among the Musgroves. He treats Anne with cold indifference, leading her to the conclusion that he no longer loves her. He flirts instead with Louisa and Henrietta, who are quite smitten with him. The party meets Captain and Mrs Harville, friends of Captain Wentworth, and Captain Benwick at Lyme. On one of their walks, they encounter a gentleman who openly admires Anne – he is later discovered to be William Elliot, Sir Walter's estranged heir. When Louisa takes a bad fall, Anne directs the others how to care for her. The Harvilles nurse Louisa over the next few months.

Anne and Lady Russell join Sir Walter and Elizabeth in Bath. They learn that Mr Elliot is there and has made great efforts to reconcile with the family. He is universally charming and continues to express great admiration for Anne, who finds him well-mannered though lacking in warmth. Admiral and Mrs Croft arrive in Bath with the surprising news that Louisa is engaged to Captain Benwick and Henrietta to Charles Hayter, her cousin. Captain Wentworth is completely unattached; he arrives in Bath soon after, and it becomes evident that he is jealous of Mr Elliot's attentions towards Anne.

During her time at Bath, Anne reconnects with an old school friend, Mrs Smith, who has fallen on hard times. The crippled, impoverished and widowed Mrs Smith informs her of Mr Elliot's dark past: he betrayed Mrs Smith's husband and wronged Mrs Smith financially, and he now plans to marry Anne because he is fearful that he will lose the baronetcy if Mrs Clay marries Sir Walter, and the marriage to Anne would ensure his inheritance. Anne is appalled.

Captain Wentworth writes a letter professing his continued devotion to Anne. Anne is stunned; they renew their engagement. William Elliot is shocked and disappointed; he leaves Bath with Mrs Clay, whose affections he has turned away from Sir Walter. Anne and Captain Wentworth finally marry. The brilliance of *Persuasion* lies in how it handles mistakes and offers second chances; it presents a heroine whose steadfastness has been costly and a hero, in Wentworth, who must negotiate anger and disappointment in order to find his way to a mature love. It is a song of experience which shows that love is a beautiful, testing and tested work that rightly makes demands on us for a lifetime.

Give us grace, Almighty Father, so to pray, as to deserve to be heard, to address thee with our Hearts, as with our lips. Thou art every where present, from Thee no secret can be hid. May the knowledge of this, teach us to fix our Thoughts on Thee, with Reverence and Devotion that we pray not in vain. Amen.

JANE AUSTEN

Day 1

It is a truth universally acknowledged, that a single man in possession of a good fortune, must be in want of a wife.

However little known the feelings or views of such a man may be on his first entering a neighbourhood, this truth is so well fixed in the minds of the surrounding families, that he is considered as the rightful property of some one or other of their daughters. *(Pride and Prejudice*, chapter 1)

The opening lines of *Pride and Prejudice* are justly famous. They are laced both with wit and a devastatingly clear-sighted encapsulation of the social constraints that applied to upper-middle-class English society in the early nineteenth century. In the 1995 BBC adaptation, these words are said by Lizzy Bennet, who delivers them with ironic relish in response to her mother's undisguised excitement that a single man 'with five thousand a year' has recently moved into the neighbourhood.

The wittiness of these opening words lies in the multiple readings they hold. Is it a truth universally acknowledged? Not necessarily. Leaving aside the class horizons – the views of the labouring classes are treated as quite irrelevant in the Bennets' genteel middle-class society – it is not clear that a single wealthy man would necessarily be in want of a wife. He might, for example, be in the country for sport. Nothing at this point is known of him. However, when placed in the ruthless economics of English upper-middle-class culture, the truth claims of the opening line are surely self-evident. In that world, marrying well was the best that could be aspired to by respectable young women and such arrangements were crucial for the maintenance of social respectability. As we discover, such is the relative precariousness of Mr and Mrs Bennet's situation that the arrival of a wealthy single man is just cause for excitement. The Bennets may be gentry, but without a male heir to secure the manor and with little financial power to tempt young men to pay mind to their daughters, they are in rather difficult straits.

The use of 'property' in this context is intriguing: 'this truth is so well fixed in the minds of the surrounding families, that he is considered as the rightful property of some one or other of their daughters'. Property may of course mean some quality or distinctive character always present in a person or group, but more familiarly, property refers to real estate or capital; it is that which we possess. In eighteenth-century England, when a woman married, she forfeited her rights to any property that was hers; she and her husband became one 'male' economic unit, with control over all her assets ceded to her husband. It is worth reminding ourselves that Georgian people were serious about love. Love was a signal of civility and culture. Those who could marry for love were civilized. Nonetheless, marriage, in at least one sense, was a property transaction. Perhaps Austen's line offers us a vision of a 'counter transaction': in a good marriage (that is, financially and socially secure), a woman gains another kind of property – a wealthy man.

The Bible is not univocal on the matter of marriage and relationships, despite some Christians insisting to the contrary. It contains a whole range of relationships that are called marriage and not all of those models are wholesome or would suit a modern temperament. When we contextualize the nature of middle-class marriage in Austen's era, it is perhaps easier to comprehend the imbalances and injustices of a property-driven marriage model. Perhaps we grasp even more firmly why marrying for love in such a culture matters: there is so very much at stake.

How do we view one another, whether we be married, partnered or single? What is the nature of our social relations and our priorities as we dwell in them? If the Bible holds within it a range of models of relationship – from the faithful, outrageously committed friendship between Naomi and Ruth and the covenantal devotion of Jonathan and David through to more familiar marriage relationships – there is, I think, a profound invitation in Christ not to regard one's partner, lover or friend in transactional or instrumental terms. Even in his Letter to Philemon, which speaks of sending a slave Onesimus back to Philemon, St Paul offers a discreet critique of that most transactional bond: slavery. He argues that Philemon, the Christian slave owner, needs to treat Onesimus, the runaway, as he would Paul. In a society in which slavery was endemic, Philemon could have put Onesimus to death. Rather, Paul invites Philemon into a new Christian vision in which Onesimus becomes a beloved brother. Such an invitation, one hopes, offered a route – in a slaving society – both to building new horizons of holy friendship and, quietly, to subverting and destroying slaving relationships.

In our context, most of us set off on relationships, marriages, friendships and life with the very best motives and intentions. Love – which is so much more than a romantic notion – is about growing into the likeness of Christ. It is an action and a work of will and a way of being in the world rather than an emotion. Even the most wonderful marriages, partnerships and relationships can resolve themselves into transactions, driven by selfishness and exploitation. Transaction can be difficult to guard against. Lent offers an opportunity to reappraise our assumptions and hopes about our relationships. As we set off on this Lenten pilgrimage, we have opportunities to ask key questions about our relationship with God, with self and with those whom we love: how do we reorientate our relationships so that they become ever more life-giving? When is it time to begin again? And crucially: how can Christ set us free to be more fully ourselves within our relationships? Ultimately, what is the deep truth we wish to see universally acknowledged in our society today?

God of Love, you call us into the likeness of Christ. Lead me, by your grace, into your ways of mercy, hope and peace. Amen.

Day 2

'[I]t has been the study of my life to avoid those weaknesses which often expose a strong understanding to ridicule.'

'Such as vanity and pride.'

'Yes, vanity is a weakness indeed. But pride – where there is a real superiority of mind, pride will be always under good regulation.'

Elizabeth turned away to hide a smile.

'Your examination of Mr. Darcy is over, I presume,' said Miss Bingley; 'and pray what is the result?'

'I am perfectly convinced by it that Mr. Darcy has no defect. He owns it himself without disguise.'

'No,' said Darcy, 'I have made no such pretension. I have faults enough, but they are not, I hope, of understanding. My temper I dare not vouch for. It is, I believe, too little yielding – certainly too little for the convenience of the world. I cannot forget the follies and vices of others so soon as I ought, nor their offences against myself. My feelings are not puffed about with every attempt to move them. My temper would perhaps be called resentful. My good opinion once lost is lost for ever.'

'That is a failing indeed!' cried Elizabeth. 'Implacable resentment is a shade in a character. But you have chosen your fault well. I really cannot laugh at it. You are safe from me.'

'There is, I believe, in every disposition a tendency to some particular evil, a natural defect, which not even the best education can overcome.'

'And your defect is a propensity to hate everybody.'

'And yours,' he replied with a smile, 'is wilfully to misunderstand them.' (*Pride and Prejudice*, chapter 11)

This encounter between Lizzy and Darcy unfolds in one of those quintessential Austen spaces for social exchange, a drawing-room. Lizzy is staying briefly at Netherfield, Mr Bingley's country house. She is there to help her sister Jane recover from a cold. Darcy and Lizzy have, for the first time, an opportunity to consider if their first impressions of one another are correct. This encounter is charged with wit and misunderstanding, as well as both Darcy's surety in himself and Lizzy's intellectual clarity. As Darcy reads, Miss Bingley – haughty and self-regarding and sensing in Lizzy a rival – invites Lizzy to take a promenade around the room. It becomes clear that Miss Bingley's intention is to attract the attention of Mr Darcy. It works. However, Miss Bingley rapidly loses her advantage. It is Darcy and Lizzy and their spiky exchange that takes centre-stage.

I am fascinated by Darcy's confidence, underscored by a seemingly forensic self-analysis. Darcy asserts, 'It has been the study of my life to avoid those weaknesses which often expose a strong understanding to ridicule.' Lizzy is inclined to mock Darcy for his pomposity and offers him an inviting trip hazard: 'Such as vanity and pride.' Darcy, however, seems oblivious and powers through: 'Yes, vanity is a weakness indeed. But pride – where there is a real superiority of mind, pride will be always under good regulation.'

Pride, of course, is one of the seven deadly sins, and the most serious one. It is the root of all evil and the beginning of sin. In *Mere Christianity*, C. S. Lewis calls it the 'anti-God state'. Pride is a dangerously corrupt selfishness, putting one's own desires and urges before the welfare of others. Dante defines pride as 'love of self perverted to hatred and contempt for one's neighbour'. Darcy is sophisticated and educated enough to recognize that unregulated pride is disastrous. Nonetheless, the modern reader is, perhaps, surprised to hear Darcy speak in such sure terms about pride as a disposition available to an essentially virtuous man. However, Darcy has the justified confidence of one of England's great landowners; a man who has been formed in the classical virtues, who exercises real power. He genuinely is a man of position and lives in a society where he can, of right, say that God has placed him in his station in life.

Of course, Darcy is not without self-awareness. He acknowledges – using the language of the era – that any disposition has weaknesses: 'There is, I believe, in every disposition a tendency to some particular evil – a natural defect, which not even the best education can overcome.' He knows he has a temperáment ('temper') that does not readily bend to the whims and needs of being liked. He suggests that 'my good opinion once lost, is lost forever'. I think Darcy's approach is more than a little alien to the mood of our own. Pride is a word that resonates negatively for many Christians. For others, both of faith and of none, pride has been reclaimed as a token of self-acceptance, resistance and solidarity by those of us who belong to traditionally marginalized 'groupings', including women, LGBTQ+ people, Global Majority Heritage, disabled etc. Pride is not necessarily a sin, if you've spent your whole life yielding to others. Darcy, a Christian of course, presents a different challenge: his pride is located in the space of the well-regulated mind sure of its place in the world.

Lizzy suggests that Darcy's defect 'is to hate everybody'. His counter is telling: 'And yours ... is wilfully to misunderstand them.' The exchange reveals how rapidly first impressions can harden into severe judgement. At this early stage in *Pride and Prejudice*, neither Darcy nor Lizzy is prepared to allow the other 'in'; each has a strong sense of who they are, but has yet to come to a mature appreciation of what they can learn about who they truly are when they are in the hands of a beloved. Those who exercise power and privilege always risk becoming conceited and supercilious. This is a profound risk for us as much as for Darcy. At the novel's close, he admits that, 'As a child I was taught what was right, but I was not taught to correct my temper. I was given good principles, but left to follow them in pride and conceit.' When we exercise privilege, there can be little to temper our sense that we are precisely where we should be. Perhaps our awareness that Darcy's early formation was inadequate might incline us to be kinder to him than not.

I suspect that few, if any, who read this book exercise privilege and position on the scale of a Darcy. However, when we place our lives in a world context, many of us hold extreme levels of privilege and power. Lent offers an opportunity for deep examination of our complacency, pride and the subtle ways in which conceit grows within. The treasures of heaven, about which Jesus speaks, are surely not conceit, complacency and condescension. They include compassion, hope and the service that draws the world into the arc of justice. Our self-examination need not be paralysing; rather, as we examine those currents that have formed us, there is an invitation from God to re-align with his ways. I don't think we ever become so fixed as creatures that our 'tempers' cannot be moderated or corrected. Darcy claims, 'My good opinion once lost, is lost forever.' We discover as the novel unfolds that Darcy does not know himself as well as he thinks. For us, Lent provides an opportunity to centre our lives on the call to grow into the likeness of Jesus Christ. The mirror of God, which is so often revealed in our relationships with our nearest and most beloved, offers a telling place for self-examination.

God of Truth, you judge your world with love. Help me to centre my life on you and dwell in your love. Amen.

Day 3

Mr. Collins was not a sensible man, and the deficiency of nature had been but little assisted by education or society; the greatest part of his life having been spent under the guidance of an illiterate and miserly father; and though he belonged to one of the universities, he had merely kept the necessary terms, without forming at it any useful acquaintance. The subjection in which his father had brought him up had given him originally great humility of manner, but it was now a good deal counteracted by the self-conceit of a weak head, living in retirement, and the consequential feelings of early and unexpected prosperity. A fortunate chance had recommended him to Lady Catherine de Bourgh when the living of Hunsford was vacant; and the respect which he felt for her high rank and his veneration for her as his patroness, mingling with a very good opinion of himself, of his authority as a clergyman, and his rights as a rector, made him altogether a mixture of pride and obsequiousness, self-importance and humility. (*Pride and Prejudice*, chapter 15)

Not least among the reasons why Jane Austen is no longer simply a novelist but an industry, is the truly sensational 1995 adaptation of *Pride and Prejudice*. It remains endlessly watchable. David Bamber's portrayal of the obsequious Mr Collins is next-level stuff. It is impossible not to read him as oily, deferential and downright ridiculous. This is Bamber's doing.

This is not the place to seek to redeem Mr Collins.[1] He is not,

---

1 For a neat, witty and subtle reading of Mr Collins in Austen's text, see Jem Bloomfield's 2014 blogpost, 'Rereading Austen: The Pride of Mr Collins', *quiteirregular*, 16 November, https://quiteirregular.wordpress.com/2014/11/16/rereading-austen-the-pride-of-mr-collins/ (accessed 24.12.2022).

as Austen flatly states, a sensible man and neither education nor experience has remedied that. Upon hearing of Collins's imminent visit to Longbourn, Lizzy says, 'He must be an oddity, I think … I cannot make him out. – There is something very pompous in his stile … Can he be a sensible man, sir?' Mr Bennet naughtily responds, 'No, my dear; I think not. I have great hopes of finding him quite the reverse.'

Given that Austen was a child of the Rectory, it is hardly surprising that her novels chew on a feast of clergymen. A reminder, however: Austen's clergy are, for the most part, scions of the gentry for whom a living offers a way for them to pursue, within reason, the life of a gentleman. The obligations placed on the clergy to hatch, match and despatch their parishioners were often undertaken by paid curates rather than those who held the living. While Austen's novels take place in the era when Evangelical enthusiasm was on the rise, her clergy are not, obviously, of that brand. They are the agents of good rural order.

Perhaps this is part of what makes Mr Collins so interesting. Not only is he quite obviously excessively servile in his devotion to his great patroness, Lady Catherine, but he has a strangely inflated sense of his place, *qua* clergyman, in society. He is caught between obsequiousness and pomposity. Lizzy is puzzled by 'his extraordinary deference for Lady Catherine' and his need to point out 'his kind intention of christening, marrying, and burying his parishioners whenever it were required'. He is not – as any good and virtuous and well-brought-up lady would ask of a cleric – 'sensible'. He comes across as too full of unregulated emotion. He has, seemingly, an excess of sensibility. Might he even be – to use it in its classic sense – an enthusiast? Might he even be on the edge of displaying and performing his piety in the manner of an Evangelical? Perhaps that would be a claim too far.

Collins, of course, goes on to prove himself a silly and often excruciating person. We might read him as a romantic foil for Darcy: while Darcy is – ultimately – the right partner for Lizzy, it is Collins whom Mrs Bennet initially wishes her to marry.

Mrs Bennet might – not unreasonably – wish Lizzy and Collins to marry to save Longbourn for the family; yet Mrs Bennet has no judgement. Collins's need to brag about his patroness's house is embarrassing *in extremis* and his servility is only matched by his complacency. He seeks to marry in haste, primarily to please his patroness; when he realizes that Jane Bennet is unavailable and Lizzy has rejected him, he settles on Lizzy's best friend, Charlotte Lucas. When Lizzy comes to stay at Hunsford, Collins can't avoid getting in a dig about what Lizzy has missed out on. His solecisms, social crassness and examples of obsequiousness go on and on. If Austen wished to take a pop at the state of the Georgian church, Collins would be 'exhibit A'.

Perhaps Collins is an example of a person with too little pride and self-respect. I wonder whether, when we read him on those terms, he becomes something less of a caricature. If Darcy's character reveals the impact of too much pride, Collins reveals what a deficit of pride looks like. This is certainly an intriguing prism through which to read him, a prism full of spiritual and theological implications. Pride – as a deadly sin – is clearly to be avoided. Should Collins's relative lack of pride be a kind of model for people of faith? Clearly not. There is such a thing as appropriate pride in self, which is usually rendered as self-respect and self-esteem. Crawling around and putting yourself down is not a mode of humility; it is a recipe for failure in well-regulated love of self. Jesus says, 'Love your neighbour as you love yourself.' All too often many of us forget the second half of this command.

Collins also has a genius for bragging. He loves the glow of patronal condescension. He loves to claim the preference of a great lady who can afford an enormous chimney. It is silly, but how many of us in our own age get a little ego-drunk when we can claim adjacency and acquaintance with minor celebrities or the great and the good? I have deployed – to my shame – more than the occasional 'humble brag' on social media, in which I state *oh so modestly* 'how honoured' I've been to be asked to be in the company of X, Y or Z, or have been asked to deliver a prestigious lecture, and so on. Ours is a show-off age where, if we're not showing off conspicuous consumption, we love to demonstrate our connections. The distorting mirror of social media can turn anyone into a show-off. When one has a lack of pride, such displays only become more tempting.

In what lies our hope? I can take hold of no stronger hope than coming to the clearest and most honest appreciation of myself and others. This requires an ever-deepening relationship with God, as well as the courage to abandon comparison and gradation. In the eyes of God we are deeply beloved and not because of our connections or achievements or position. For women in particular, I think there is a greater call: to overcome the expectation that we are 'made' for service and subservience in a way men are not. It requires us to claim self-respect and an appropriate pride that subverts much that religion and culture teach us. It entails claiming space and saying we belong in those spaces. At the deepest level, though, the hope of growing into our fullest selves – which is what humility really is – lies in a letting go: of the crass separateness and individualism that centres 'me', 'ego', 'self' as the central character in the drama. We all play walk-on parts and this is a beautiful thing.

Loving God, abide with me today. Show us the way to true humility through your Son Jesus Christ. Amen.

Day 4

'I am ill-qualified to recommend myself to strangers.'

'Shall we ask your cousin the reason of this?' said Elizabeth, still addressing Colonel Fitzwilliam. 'Shall we ask him why a man of sense and education, and who has lived in the world, is ill qualified to recommend himself to strangers?'

'I can answer your question,' said Fitzwilliam, 'without applying to him. It is because he will not give himself the trouble.'

'I certainly have not the talent which some people possess,' said Darcy, 'of conversing easily with those I have never seen before. I cannot catch their tone of conversation, or appear interested in their concerns, as I often see done.'

'My fingers,' said Elizabeth, 'do not move over this instrument in the masterly manner which I see so many women's do … But then I have always supposed it to be my own fault – because I would not take the trouble of practising. It is not that I do not believe *my* fingers as capable as any other woman's of superior execution.'

Darcy smiled and said, 'You are perfectly right. You have employed your time much better. No one admitted to the privilege of hearing you can think any thing wanting. We neither of us perform to strangers.' (*Pride and Prejudice*, chapter 31)

When Lizzy and Darcy meet at Rosings, the home of Darcy's aunt, the imperious Lady Catherine De Bourgh, their relationship continues to crackle with mistrust and misunderstanding. Lizzy is convinced that Darcy has mistreated the charming Mr Wickham, the son of the steward of Darcy's father; she is also sure that Darcy sought to disengage his friend Mr Bingley from his attachment to her sister Jane. During an evening at Rosings, as Lizzy plays the piano – with Darcy's cousin Colonel Fitz-william for an audience – Mr Darcy approaches her. Unknown to Lizzy, Darcy has fallen in love with her; she imagines that his approach signals his desire to lock horns. Indeed, she says, 'You mean to frighten me ... by coming in all this state to hear me?' Darcy denies he has any such intent, teasing her by saying, 'I have had the pleasure of your acquaintance long enough to know that you find great enjoyment in occasionally professing opin-ions which in fact are not your own.' With Colonel Fitzwilliam as witness, Lizzy playfully gives an account of Darcy's haughty and unsocial behaviour while in Hertfordshire with Bingley; the tone is light, but it has edge. Lizzy would not be so distasteful as to directly accuse Darcy of treating Mr Wickham infamously or of detaching Bingley from Jane. Nonetheless, she speaks of how Darcy barely danced at the Assembly in Meryton despite a short-age of male partners; Darcy retorts that he knew no one beyond his own party. The sexual and social tension is palpable.

Leaving aside the social obligations of Regency upper-middle-class culture for a moment, I am inclined to have more than a little sympathy with Darcy's seeming social awkwardness. 'I am ill-qualified to recommend myself to strangers' is a line I've often wished to deploy in conversation. Like many people, I am more than capable of projecting myself into a roomful of people if that is my role or job. However, my actual disposition at a party is to find one person, ideally someone I already know, and settle down for a proper chat.

Colonel Fitzwilliam offers an alternative explanation for Darcy's lack of social proaction: 'It is because he will not give himself the trouble.' Darcy, the man of good principles, has perhaps grown into a man who will not make the efforts required by social obligation. We come then to the decisive exchange in this encounter between Darcy and Lizzy. Darcy acknowledges that he has not the talent that some people possess of conversing easily with those they do not know. Is Darcy throwing 'shade' over Lizzy's favourite, Mr Wickham, a man of easy manners? Almost certainly. Elizabeth's retort is devastating: 'My fingers,' said Elizabeth, 'do not move over this instrument in the masterly manner which I see so many women's do ... But then I have always supposed it to be my own fault – because I would not take the trouble of practising.'

Lizzy's words speak powerfully into the Christian vocation to discipleship and formation. Aristotle suggested that humans are primarily creatures of habit and practice; we are, ultimately, what we do most. Flowing out of this, via St Thomas Aquinas, is a tradition which says that the virtuous life – the life growing into the likeness of Christ – is a habit-shaped and habit-forming life. I both take great comfort and find great challenge in that. The comfort lies in the sense that if I am to become more Christ-like I can bring my energy and commitment to it; in the midst of God's grace, I am not doomed to failure. I may practise and be formed. The challenge lies in the need for commitment. Yet, as Jesus reminds us, we are called to love God and neighbour with our whole heart, body, soul and mind. We are called to be 'all in'. While I am sure that God looks upon us with delight and encouragement, I believe in the power of pilgrimage, and pilgrimage requires the will and courage to step out of the door, to commit. The good news is that prayer and pilgrimage do not have to have the lonely, determined character of a young person grinding out scales in order to become a virtuoso. It can and ought to be undertaken in the company of others.

I love that line of Darcy's: 'We neither of us perform to strangers.' It contains a quiet dignity that resists the theatrical urge to make a show or turn on one's personality to win a room or a crowd or a theatre. It asserts a trust in the intimate, the true intimacy of relationships tested over time in friendship or family. If it is a conservative assertion, it is one that challenges us in our attention-driven age. A friend once quipped that 'attention is my love language'; well, in an era driven by Instagram and TikTok, giving and receiving attention is pretty much everyone's love language. I'm not sure that this is necessarily bad. However, in the economy and ecology of God lies an invitation into a simpler, more intimate relationship; not with the many who shower applause (and in due course sometimes reject savagely), but with the One who is faithful, gracious and loving. In his presence we have no need to make display, with either strangers or friends.

God of Pilgrimage, lead us deeper into your way of grace. When we are tempted to fall away, abide with us in your Son, Jesus Christ. Amen.

*Incline us oh God! to think humbly of our-
selves, to be severe only in the examination
of our own conduct, to consider our fellow-
creatures with kindness, and to judge of all
they say and do with that charity which we
would desire from them ourselves. Amen.*

JANE AUSTEN

Day 5

'In vain have I struggled. It will not do. My feelings will not be repressed. You must allow me to tell you how ardently I admire and love you.'

Elizabeth's astonishment was beyond expression. She stared, coloured, doubted, and was silent. This he considered sufficient encouragement, and the avowal of all that he felt and had long felt for her immediately followed. He spoke well, but there were feelings besides those of the heart to be detailed, and he was not more eloquent on the subject of tenderness than of pride. His sense of her inferiority – of its being a degradation – of the family obstacles which judgment had always opposed to inclination, were dwelt on with a warmth which seemed due to the consequence he was wounding, but was very unlikely to recommend his suit. ... when he ceased, the colour rose into her cheeks, and she said,

'In such cases as this, it is, I believe, the established mode to express a sense of obligation for the sentiments avowed, however unequally they may be returned. It is natural that obligation should be felt, and if I could *feel* gratitude, I would now thank you. But I cannot – I have never desired your good opinion, and you have certainly bestowed it most unwillingly. I am sorry to have occasioned pain to any one. It has been most unconsciously done, however, and I hope will be of short duration. The feelings which, you tell me, have long prevented the acknowledgment of your regard, can have little difficulty in overcoming it after this explanation.' ...

At length, in a voice of forced calmness, he said,

'And this is all the reply which I am to have the honour of expecting! I might, perhaps, wish to be informed why, with so little *endeavour* at civility, I am thus rejected. But it is of small importance.'

17

'I might as well enquire,' replied she, 'why, with so evident a design of offending and insulting me, you chose to tell me that you liked me against your will, against your reason, and even against your character?' (*Pride and Prejudice*, chapter 34)

I am in awe of Lizzy in this scene: her composure, her self-awareness, and the barely controlled fury. While we later discover that part of her anger towards Darcy is based on a mistaken premise – her belief that Darcy has treated Mr Wickham infamously – Lizzy's response to the prideful, over-confident, and oh-so-privileged Darcy is one of the great romantic burns of all time.

Darcy is – to mix metaphors – simply outgunned by the righteous clarity of Lizzy. This is a feminist moment *par excellence*: here is a relatively powerless and (in terms of prospects – she's already turned down one potential husband!) vulnerable woman simply telling the great landowner to jog on. She does not observe the expected genteel form: a sense of obligation for Darcy's sentiments. Rather, with considerable justification, she responds to him as what he is: a pillock with ten thousand a year. She will not forget his prior insults to her family. She will not be treated as an inferior and I love her for it. Lizzie's conclusion is devastating:

> 'You are mistaken, Mr. Darcy, if you suppose that the mode of your declaration affected me in any other way, than as it spared me the concern which I might have felt in refusing you, had you behaved in a more gentleman-like manner. ... You could not have made me the offer of your hand in any possible way that would have tempted me to accept it ... I had not known you a month before I felt that you were the last man in the world whom I could ever be prevailed on to marry.'

Late in the novel, when Darcy and Lizzy are about to be engaged, this time as equals and as changed beings, Darcy recalls what he takes as her most devastating line: 'Your reproof, so well applied, I shall never forget: "had you behaved in a more gentleman-like manner." Those were your words. You know not, you can scarcely conceive, how they have tortured me; though it was some time, I confess, before I was reasonable enough to allow their justice.'

Pride and Prejudice offers both Lizzy and Darcy time and opportunity to be 're-formed'. For Lizzy, there is a re-visioning of reality in which she comes clearly to perceive the facts hiding beneath her prejudices. Darcy comes to a reformulation of his self-understanding. He sees himself as that most desirable thing in his society: a gentleman. Yet his behaviour speaks otherwise. Few, if any, of us are free of 'personal myths' and distorted 'self-understandings'. None of us are the complete article in this life, except Jesus Christ. At one level, Darcy's proposal and Lizzy's rejoinder constitute a reminder – in Darcy's case – to 'check his privilege', and – in Lizzy's – to check the facts. Lizzy's misperceptions about Darcy begin to be addressed quite quickly: he is able to refute Mr Wickham's false account of himself in the letter that he writes to Lizzie immediately after the proposal. The work of 'checking his privilege' – which is nothing short of getting a greater grip on who he actually is and how he is in the world – is a slower work.

I believe that the work of dwelling deeply in God's hope and love unfolds slowly. Rarely do the important and abiding changes in character happen in a flash. The vocation to love has to be negotiated through the line of the body, in real time and often with great soul-searching and pain. It is the slow work of God. It may well entail apology and, more often than not, the seeking after forgiveness and reconciliation, as well as a fair amount of cringe, embarrassment and indeed a reckoning with shame. Like Darcy, we might say of our old ways and behaviours, 'I assure you that I have long been most heartily ashamed of it.' We might become Christians in a flash, but conversion to the ways of God is a lifetime's work of attention.

You should not lose heart, of course. Consider Darcy's second declaration of love, late in the novel (Chapter 58). It is humble and hopeful and never for a moment forgets that the one whom

he is addressing is an actual person with liberty and a beating
heart:

> After a short pause, her companion added, 'You are too gen-
> erous to trifle with me. If your feelings are still what they were
> last April, tell me so at once. *My* affections and wishes are
> unchanged, but one word from you will silence me on this
> subject for ever.'
>
> Elizabeth, feeling all the more than common awkwardness
> and anxiety of his situation, now forced herself to speak;
> and immediately, though not very fluently, gave him to un-
> derstand that her sentiments had undergone so material a
> change, since the period to which he alluded, as to make her
> receive with gratitude and pleasure his present assurances.
> The happiness which this reply produced, was such as he had
> probably never felt before; and he expressed himself on the
> occasion as sensibly and as warmly as a man violently in love
> can be supposed to do. Had Elizabeth been able to encounter
> his eye, she might have seen how well the expression of heart-
> felt delight, diffused over his face, became him; but, though
> she could not look, she could listen, and he told her of feel-
> ings, which, in proving of what importance she was to him,
> made his affection every moment more valuable.

*Fearless God, you show us the way to abundant life in Jesus
Christ, your Son. Fill my heart this day with love, and a longing
to follow him. Amen.*

Day 6

'This will not do,' said Elizabeth. 'You never will be able to make both of them good for any thing. Take your choice, but you must be satisfied with only one. There is but such a quantity of merit between them; just enough to make one good sort of man; and of late it has been shifting about pretty much. For my part, I am inclined to believe it all Mr. Darcy's, but you shall do as you choose.'

It was some time, however, before a smile could be extorted from Jane.

'I do not know when I have been more shocked,' said she. 'Wickham so very bad! It is almost past belief. And poor Mr Darcy! dear Lizzy, only consider what he must have suffered. Such a disappointment! and with the knowledge of your ill opinion too! and having to relate such a thing of his sister! It is really too distressing. I am sure you must feel it so.'

'Oh! no, my regret and compassion are all done away by seeing you so full of both. I know you will do him such ample justice, that I am growing every moment more unconcerned and indifferent. Your profusion makes me saving; and if you lament over him much longer, my heart will be as light as a feather.'

'Poor Wickham; there is such an expression of goodness in his countenance! such an openness and gentleness in his manner.'

'There certainly was some great mismanagement in the education of those two young men. One has got all the goodness, and the other all the appearance of it.' (*Pride and Prejudice*, chapter 40)

Jane Bennet is beautiful, generous and good humoured. As Mr Bennet says of her and her future husband Bingley, 'You are each of you so complying, that nothing will ever be resolved on; so easy, that every servant will cheat you; and so generous, that you will always exceed your income.' In essence, she is disposed to understand others, even Mr Wickham, and see the best in them.

As Jane and Lizzy become aware of their mistakes regarding the characters of Darcy and Wickham, Jane faces questions about her judgement. Some who read *Pride and Prejudice* might say that it is hardly surprising that Jane struggles to read reality aright: she is barely 20 and hardly versed in the cruelties of the world. She is, in addition, lacking in the sass and intellectual vigour of Lizzy. Her desire to read good manners and a pleasing countenance as tokens of inner goodness is naive. However, she is not the first or last person to confuse beauty with truth.

It might be tempting to act as if we are superior to Jane in our judgements about the characters of others. Certainly, I – like many – want to insist that experience has taught me not to believe that beauty and charm are the same as truth. As Hamlet says, 'a man may smile and smile, and be a villain'. I have spent sufficient time in the world of church politics to say that I have met people who are wonderfully polite, warm and lovely to my face, yet hold views which would gladly see my kind – LGBTQ+, etc. – ejected from leadership in the Church. In one sense, I much prefer those people who are honest in their antipathies. However, I think we are foolish if we act as if we are above making false judgements about others or reality. I think the moment we think we are too smart or cynical to make such errors of judgement is the point we are most likely to be tricked. It has happened to me in various ways. For example, because of my sympathy towards a particular bias, or my fondness for or trust in certain people or social media accounts, I've shared links which – when I've engaged my brain and investigative sense – have been revealed to contain, at best, half-truths. Any of us can get scammed, not least because any of us can become passionate about an issue or are flustered in the moment or haven't engaged our brains and so on.

At the outset of Lent, we often hear that passage from Matthew 6 in which Jesus talks about where our treasure is. He also asks us, when we pray, to go into our room and pray to the Father who is unseen. This image holds for me a deeply attractive quietude. It invites me to pray in secret to the God who is known in secret. I don't think this should be read as some sort of practice for a special class of initiates; rather, it captures how powerful space and quiet and discernment can be when it comes to making wise and sustainable judgements. Sometimes we are required to make decisions in a hurry. However, more often than not we only think we are so required. Equally, when that time of crisis comes, to have built up our prayerful judgement through time spent with God will bear richer fruit. None of us – not Jane or Lizzy Bennet or you or me – has 20/20 judgement regarding the changing scenes and demands of life. However, to take time to prayerfully examine what lies behind the appearance of goodness (or seeming wickedness) and come to a better grip on the facts will rarely lead us astray. Perhaps, today, you or I will face an urgent judgement call or a pressing need for action. Probably we won't. However, if we do, by what criteria shall we discern between urgent and important? What difference is made when we take up God's invitation to inhabit prayerful space with him? How might responding to that invitation make the world a more hopeful place?

Almighty God, help us to locate our deepest treasure in you. Teach us to love you with our whole heart, mind, body and soul. Amen.

Day 7

'His manners are very different from his cousin's.'

'Yes, very different. But I think Mr. Darcy improves upon acquaintance.'

'Indeed!' cried Wickham with a look which did not escape her. 'And pray, may I ask?' but checking himself, he added, in a gayer tone, 'Is it in address that he improves? Has he deigned to add aught of civility to his ordinary style? – for I dare not hope,' he continued in a lower and more serious tone, 'that he is improved in essentials.'

'Oh, no!' said Elizabeth. 'In essentials, I believe, he is very much what he ever was.'

While she spoke, Wickham looked as if scarcely knowing whether to rejoice over her words, or to distrust their meaning. There was a something in her countenance which made him listen with an apprehensive and anxious attention, while she added: 'When I said that he improved on acquaintance, I did not mean that his mind or his manners were in a state of improvement, but that, from knowing him better, his disposition was better understood.' (*Pride and Prejudice*, chapter 41)

If Lizzy's time at Rosings has not entirely disposed her to view Darcy with fondness, it has removed the scales from her eyes regarding the well-mannered but untrustworthy Mr Wickham. As Wickham's regiment prepares to move from Meryton to Brighton, he continues to shine his charm in Lizzy's direction. She is, at this point, totally resilient to it; Wickham's obvious social gifts begin to be overshadowed by Darcy's truth. Lizzy is in total control of this encounter with Wickham. Her wit – capable of being read in multiple directions – exposes Wickham's reliance on a false narrative about the world. She says, of Darcy, 'In essentials, I believe, he is very much what he ever was.' Wickham is clever enough to realize that Lizzy may now be better acquainted with the truth about his bad conduct and disposition, but is so totally invested in his lying that he can neither be honest with Lizzy nor quite believe that he is on the edge of exposure. Lizzy's words do not offer him any further reassurance.

How do we distinguish between what is essential and inessential in a person's character or identity? If – guilty confession time – you've listened to as many 'true crime' podcasts as me, you will have come across the phenomenon of the person who, though they commit a quite heinous crime, says, 'It wasn't me. I am not that person.' They act a little like Leonardo DiCaprio's character in the film *Shutter Island* whose 'personal myth' insists that they are a good person, perhaps even a hero, rather than a monster. At most, they can only accept their wicked action as an aberration.

John 16.13 says, 'When the Spirit of truth comes, he will guide you into all the truth; for he will not speak on his own, but will speak whatever he hears, and he will declare to you the things that are to come.' Truth, though, is rarely revealed as a kind of fact or piece of propositional knowledge. We do not get it all at once, nor as a series of facts and assertions. Time and relationship matter. Who you are and who others are is revealed in relationship across time. That is part of the power and beauty of Austen's writing: revelations about human goodness and promise, as much as self-centredness and cupidity, emerge in recognizable human situations. I believe that humans can change, even as we grow older. The theory that our ability to change lessens over time, 'neuroplasticity', only takes us so far. Being in the company of Jesus Christ is transformative, though I do find myself more inclined to be fixed in my opinions the older I become. Nonetheless, the invitation to grow into the likeness of Christ is an invitation to grow and change. Some of those changes may indeed be behavioural; but they are also invitations to perceive what is there with fresh eyes.

Darcy has not changed in essentials. Lizzy, however, has come to see reality more clearly. Wickham might, at one level, be seen as a stock character of Romance, the 'cad', but his capacity to work a room and present his fictions as fact are – as we've seen with certain modern politicians – a real-life phenomenon. In our lives it can be exceptionally difficult to discern fact from fiction, reality from fantasy. The beautiful messiness of human relationships makes such judgement calls even tougher. We are affective beings as much as rational ones, and thank God for that. Attention matters, and when we are attentive to the things of life and goodness, the world opens out. As theologian Janet Martin Soskice reminds us, when we do that, 'attention is rewarded with reality'.[1]

Lent is, among other things, an opportunity to strip away the fake from the life-giving; the tasty but empty from that which actually nourishes. Lent invites us into the work of attention, and when we attend to the things of God we are rewarded with reality. We, as much as Lizzy, will discover that the facts are our friends. Sometimes they are difficult to treat with. However, as we treat with reality, we are better able to be alert to the promise and possibility, the fundamental love of Jesus Christ, woven into creation. We are able to say 'God is Love' and know we are speaking truth and touching reality; we know that such a claim is not romantic fantasy about the world. Rather, we see the world ever more as what it truly is: messy and bewildering, but longing for and tending towards the goodness and glory of God.

Father of All, you long to meet us in the wilderness of our wandering and bring us home. Lead me into the ways of your righteousness this day. Amen.

---

1 Janet Martin Soskice, *The Kindness of God* (Oxford: Oxford University Press, 2007), p. 27.

Day 8

'Miss Bennet, ... do not expect to be noticed by his family or friends, if you wilfully act against the inclinations of all. You will be censured, slighted, and despised, by every one connected with him. Your alliance will be a disgrace; your name will never even be mentioned by any of us.'

'These are heavy misfortunes,' replied Elizabeth. 'But the wife of Mr Darcy must have such extraordinary sources of happiness necessarily attached to her situation, that she could, upon the whole, have no cause to repine.'

'Obstinate, headstrong girl! I am ashamed of you! Is this your gratitude for my attentions to you last spring? Is nothing due to me on that score? Let us sit down. You are to understand, Miss Bennet, that I came here with the determined resolution of carrying my purpose; nor will I be dissuaded from it. I have not been used to submit to any person's whims. I have not been in the habit of brooking disappointment.'

'*That* will make your ladyship's situation at present more pitiable; but it will have no effect on *me*.'

'I will not be interrupted. Hear me in silence ... The upstart pretensions of a young woman without family, connections, or fortune. Is this to be endured! But it must not, shall not be. If you were sensible of your own good, you would not wish to quit the sphere in which you have been brought up.' ...

'Whatever my connections may be,' said Elizabeth, 'if your nephew does not object to them, they can be nothing to *you*.'
(*Pride and Prejudice*, chapter 56)

Pride and Prejudice is notable for its many sparkling exchanges. However, this encounter between Lady Catherine de Bourgh and Lizzy is an absolute classic. I wish it were possible to include it in its entirety. I can make no greater recommendation than advise you to go to chapter 56 and enjoy its cut and thrust. Lady Catherine's line, as she comes to terms with the prospect of Lizzy becoming mistress of Darcy's ancestral home, is one for the ages: 'Are the shades of Pemberley to be thus polluted?'

How do we see and understand ourselves? That is surely a key question when we come to reflect on this encounter. Lady Catherine de Bourgh is not an attractive person. She teeters on the edge of being a grotesque. However, she is no pretentious bore like Mr Collins. Lady Catherine is a substantial personage. In her widowhood, she is a great and wealthy landowner, a rarity among women. She is well-connected, titled and would have operated among the great and the good. Her nephew, Darcy, is no minor gentry; though he has no title, his wealth and historic power is the match for many in the highest echelons of English society. It would be absurd for Lady Catherine not to see herself and her family as among the most exalted in the land. There are grounds for her condescension towards Lizzy. Lizzy may be the daughter of a gentleman, but Mr Bennet is of no great import. Mrs Bennet is not of the gentry class. Might it not be reasonable for Lady Catherine – in the strictly stratified reality of early nineteenth-century England – to say, 'Your alliance will be a disgrace; your name will never even be mentioned by any of us.' Lady Catherine overstates her case for effect, but she is not so far out of order. As for Lizzy, her self-understanding, always well-formed and appropriately self-critical, has been ever more clearly honed by her encounters with Wickham and her growing love for Darcy. Her awesome self-possession is such that should I ever come under the verbal assault of some over-privileged person, I hope and pray I have even half of her poise.

Lady Catherine is out of order. She dares to come into Mr Bennet's home and effectively demands to know not only Lizzy's intentions, but tries to exact a promise from her not to marry Darcy under any circumstances. Lady Catherine is used to getting her own way and treating others as props in her own drama. She has a fantasy about her own daughter marrying Darcy and is determined that it shall be so. She is so convinced by her alternative picture of reality that she even suggests that her behaviour to Lizzy the previous year at Rosings was worthy of due deference: 'Obstinate, headstrong girl! I am ashamed of you! Is this your gratitude for my attentions to you last spring? Is nothing due to me on that score?'

Lady Catherine is a character caught up in her own version of 'post-truth'. She is so very used to others accepting her account of reality that she is unwilling to treat with the truth right in front of her: that a so-called 'obstinate, headstrong girl' is precisely the right person to marry Darcy. She has become so inured to her own perspective that she simply presumes that it is the right one. Lady Catherine is a kind of autocrat, unable to accept and rejoice in the realities (perhaps even the democracy) of the heart. Of course, we do not ultimately know her long-term response to Lizzy and Darcy's union. *Pride and Prejudice* does not record it. In *Death Comes To Pemberley*, P. D. James speculates that over time Lady Catherine comes to respect, perhaps even love, her nephew's bride.

I think many of us have drawn close to 'doing a Lady Catherine'. I am certainly inclined to an overweening sense that my 'take' on any number of things is the correct one. My sense is that we are living in the age of what the political theorist Moises Naim calls 'polarization'; that is, of great division and the flight to extremes, in which those who disagree cannot find common ground. He suggests that social media algorithms only feed this flight to polar opposites; they drive us towards more and more extreme versions of what we've been fed before. I have never lived through a time when there has been such division and over-surety about any number of things from the direction of the UK (Brexit or not) to human identity. It can feel as if our disagreements are less to do with nuanced differences and more like dogmatic religious beliefs. I have noticed in myself a tendency towards a hardening of my views and an attendant risk of othering and dehumanizing those with whom I disagree.

I'm not suggesting that Lady Catherine is a kind of prototype of our age of polarization. However, she reminds us to be alert, in our pilgrimage of faith, not to be inattentive to grace. To follow Jesus Christ means to seek to centre our lives on him. If we are talking the language of 'poles' and 'polarization', Jesus is True North. He also offers us the route map to dwell ever more deeply in God. Part of that requires a preparedness to let go, as well as to pray for our enemies. The letting go is about finding your life not in social media 'likes', approbation and celebrity, or in position and power, but in taking up the cross and following Jesus. It is about finding your life beyond the sureties of your own opinion. Praying for our enemies might seem to be just an exercise in pouring hot coals on those who've hurt us or who have demonstrated abiding wickedness. It can be that. At other times it is an invitation to keep those whom we treat as vile, lesser or not part of our tribe in the gracious spotlight of the Living God. When we do that, we take the risk of stepping into that spotlight too.

Humble God, in Jesus Christ you entered this world as one who serves. Grant me this day the grace to love and serve as he loved all. Amen.

Day 9

'I have been a selfish being all my life, in practice, though not in principle. As a child I was taught what was *right*, but I was not taught to correct my temper. I was given good principles, but left to follow them in pride and conceit. Unfortunately an only son (for many years an only *child*), I was spoilt by my parents, who, though good themselves (my father, particularly, all that was benevolent and amiable), allowed, encouraged, almost taught me to be selfish and overbearing; to care for none beyond my own family circle; to think meanly of all the rest of the world; to *wish* at least to think meanly of their sense and worth compared with my own. Such I was, from eight to eight and twenty; and such I might still have been but for you, dearest, loveliest Elizabeth! What do I not owe you! You taught me a lesson, hard indeed at first, but most advantageous. By you, I was properly humbled. I came to you without a doubt of my reception. You showed me how insufficient were all my pretensions to please a woman worthy of being pleased.' (*Pride and Prejudice*, chapter 58)

'By you I was properly humbled.' Humility is one of those virtues I find difficult to define. Too often when we talk about humility we mean a kind of self-abasement that gives humility a bad name. When humility is characterized as a sort of bowing and scraping, a putting yourself down, or a faked way of being in the world, *à la* Uriah Heep in *David Copperfield*, we do not properly engage with humility. Equally, humility has been used as a tool for controlling the behaviour of women: it has been treated as *the* female virtue. Humility has readily been translated into female modesty and sold to women and girls by patriarchal religion as the appropriate way to inhabit the world.

One of humility's richest etymological roots is '*humus*' or earth. It takes us back to that deep biblical truth: from dust you come and to dust you shall return. We are creatures of earth and we shall return to it. Darcy admits that he is a man who was given good principles, but left to follow them in pride and conceit; his indulgent parents allowed him to fixate on his family and position. It is through his emerging relationship with Lizzy, someone who sees through his presumptions and who is herself lacking in the privileges and power he exercises, that he is brought down to earth. He is revealed for the earth and dust he is. He is humbled, but not humiliated.

How are we to reflect on and inhabit the humility modelled by Jesus Christ? He makes any number of startling pronouncements: in Luke 9.23, he says, 'If any want to become my followers, let them deny themselves and take up their cross daily and follow me'; in Matthew 20.26–27, 'whoever wishes to be great among you must be your servant, and whoever wishes to be first among you must be your slave'. Here, surely, is an invitation towards abasement, yes? We are also invited to be perfect as our Heavenly Father is perfect. Perfection and abasement are surely a toxic combination, by turns unliveable and a guaranteed cause for shame as we inevitably fall short. However, I read Jesus' invitations as indications to 'be close to where I am' and 'grow into my likeness'. We are creatures of earth, but we are also those who bear the image of God. We are capable, by virtue of the God-Image, of being those who dwell in the abundance of God's love, grace and mercy; we too can grow into the likeness of Christ. We do that in relationship. Sometimes in specific relationships such as that of Lizzy and Darcy: as we grow into abiding, truth-filled relationships, we begin not only to lose that which gets in the way of flourishing, but also to grow into the community of love and hope. Our separateness and selfishness begin to ebb away. If that can happen in human relationship, how much more so in the company and community of the living God, whether we be happily single or partnered? As we begin to grow into Christ's likeness we want to be where he is – in service and appropriate humility.

We see that we are dust and to dust we shall return, but this does not paralyse or limit us. We are set free for life – life in this world and in the world to come.

Many years ago, I was told by a wise spiritual director that when Jesus says 'be perfect' he is not saying 'be a holier-than-thou goody two shoes' but 'be who God has called you to be'; he is calling each of us to be ourselves in all our God-given uniqueness and to dwell ever more deeply in the call to be a member of the Body of Christ. I've always taken great encouragement from that. The God who formed me in the womb does not need me to be a carbon copy of every other human being who's ever lived, nor to lead a life that is not my own, forever seeking after someone's else's life with envy or greed. Rather, I am called to be me and to find my place in the Body of Christ. That is humility: to be myself as God has called me to be. I've found that a lifetime's work. At its deepest, however, it is not about striving, but about letting go; it is about meeting and being changed by the living God. That is a vocation worth having.

Liberating God, set me free to be ever more who you call me to be. Help me to take up the cross and follow my Lord. Amen.

Day 10

'Indeed, to say the truth, I am convinced within myself that your father had no idea of your giving them any money at all. The assistance he thought of, I dare say, was only such as might be reasonably expected of you; for instance, such as looking out for a comfortable small house for them, helping them to move their things, and sending them presents of fish and game, and so forth, whenever they are in season. I'll lay my life that he meant nothing farther; indeed, it would be very strange and unreasonable if he did. Do but consider, my dear Mr Dashwood, how excessively comfortable your mother-in-law and her daughters may live on the interest of seven thousand pounds, besides the thousand pounds belonging to each of the girls, which brings them in fifty pounds a year a-piece, and, of course, they will pay their mother for their board out of it. Altogether, they will have five hundred a-year amongst them, and what on earth can four women want for more than that? They will live so cheap! Their housekeeping will be nothing at all. They will have no carriage, no horses, and hardly any servants; they will keep no company, and can have no expenses of any kind! Only conceive how comfortable they will be! Five hundred a year! I am sure I cannot imagine how they will spend half of it; and as to your giving them more, it is quite absurd to think of it. They will be much more able to give *you* something.'

'Upon my word,' said Mr Dashwood, 'I believe you are perfectly right. My father certainly could mean nothing more by his request to me than what you say. I clearly understand it now, and I will strictly fulfil my engagement by such acts of assistance and kindness to them as you have described. When my mother removes into another house my services shall be readily given to accommodate her as far as I can. Some little

34

present of furniture too may be acceptable then.' (*Sense and Sensibility*, chapter 2)

Sometimes Jane Austen's writing is hilarious. Sometimes it simultaneously carries an edge of moral critique that is as sharp as the most savage blade. The famous exchange between John and his wife Fanny is precisely one of those occasions. This short excerpt captures much of its cringey brilliance. However, it is worth reading the chapter in full and I invite you to do so. As we laugh at Fanny's ever-widening exposure of the boundlessness of her greed and her husband's ready capitulation to it, we also witness the easy way in which those who have much can rationalize giving nothing to those who have little.

The context is this: Henry Dashwood, his second wife and their three daughters, Elinor, Marianne and Margaret, have lived for many years with Henry's wealthy bachelor uncle at Norland Park. That uncle decides, in late life, to will the use and income of his property first to Henry, then to Henry's son (by his first marriage) John Dashwood, so that the property should pass intact to John's four-year-old son Harry. The uncle dies, but Henry lives just a year after that and is unable in such a short time to save enough money for the future security of his second wife and his daughters. On his deathbed, Henry extracts a promise from John to take care of his half-sisters. But barely is Henry dead before John's wife Fanny persuades her husband to renege on the promise, appealing to his concerns about diminishing his own son Harry's inheritance. This is despite the fact that John is already independently wealthy, thanks both to his inheritance from his mother and his wife's dowry. Henry Dashwood's love for his second family is also used by Fanny to arouse her husband's jealousy, and persuade him not to help his sisters financially.

The way Austen describes Fanny's determined and persistent 'talking down' of John's instinct to follow his father's wishes is a masterwork of comedy. We can almost see Fanny's mind whirring as she slowly but surely moves John from generosity to parsimony. Within a few pages, John moves from being – in principle – prepared to give the Dashwood ladies substantial support, down to offering a few sticks of furniture (duly withdrawn), until finally he arrives at permitting Mrs Dashwood to take some china crockery that she already possesses. Fanny suggests that Henry must have been delirious when he extracted a promise from John to help the soon-to-be destitute women. She reminds him that his own son will lose out and that Mrs Dashwood might live 15 years and be an endless drain on John's resources. She leads John away from generosity as she slyly notes how any money given to the Dashwood sisters will ultimately go away from the family to anyone they marry.

At one level, this is all broad-brush, deeply amusing villainy. It satisfyingly sets Fanny up as a greedy villain in contrast to the essentially good-hearted Dashwood sisters; it positions John as a labile and easily manipulated miser who will never treat his family right (further slighting the sisters later in the novel when he and Fanny invite the Steele sisters to stay with them in London, rather than his half-sisters). At a deeper level, the exchange captures the extent to which genteel Georgian women who lacked a fortune were readily caught in the jaws of ruthless and cruel social conventions and power structures. Outside of marriage, the best a genteel woman without fortune might hope for in terms of occupation was as a governess (as we witness with Jane Fairfax in *Emma*). John and Fanny effectively condemn the Dashwoods to genteel poverty. Crucially, this passage reveals that the defining state of a middle-class woman in Georgian England was dependence. The simple fact that John and Fanny Dashwood as family will not help their half-sisters and mother-in-law is a serious failure of social and familial obligation and love.

We can act as if the social conditions under which we live are more enlightened than those known in Austen's time; we can also act as if we are ethically better. As Christians, perhaps we want to align with a biblical figure like Abraham rather than Fanny: where Fanny manipulates her husband down from generosity to indifference and near cruelty, Abraham famously entreats God from judgement to generosity. In the book of

Genesis (18.21–33), we read how the righteous Abraham entreats God to save the city of Sodom. God is determined to wipe out the notoriously inhospitable place. Abraham says to God, 'Will you wipe out the righteous with the wicked?' and asks, 'If there were 50 righteous men in the city would you still destroy it?' God says no. As Abraham slowly reduces the number down from 50 to ten, he gradually negotiates God away from savage judgement to generosity. Crucially, he reminds God of who he actually is: a God whose judgements are shaped by righteousness and grace. God is gracious and generous first.

Perhaps I am a more notorious sinner than most, but I find myself tempted to be more like Fanny and John than Abraham and God. I am tempted to be greedy like Fanny. In countless little ways, I find myself deciding not to be generous; I do not respond to neighbour and stranger out of a call to grace and love. If that does not make me exactly 'greedy', I am not proud of my selfish instincts. All I know is that in the face of a world of profound need, whether on the streets where I live or in geographically distant places, I am more often than not tempted to talk myself down from my ethical obligations to love my neighbour. I am caught up in self-interest rather than being shaped by the generosity at the heart of God. I find it takes a focused and determined decision to start again and again from the truth at the heart of the world: that all we have is gift and we are called to respond in kind. All we have comes from God and of his own do we give.

Lent, certainly, should focus our minds, hearts and souls. It grants us an opportunity to centre on that which truly matters. Of course, the call of God is not simply for Lent; our obligations are not simply in force in times of Lenten fasting or, for example, when there is a pressing crisis in the world. We are called to be like the God who made us: we are called to be agents of grace and generosity and gift. Sometimes we need to be reminded about who and what we are and who we are called to be. Tempting though it is to capitulate to our inner Fanny and John Dashwood, the way of life leads us to the table of grace.

Generous God, all we have comes from you and your own do we give. Make of my life a sacrifice of praise and a gift of ever-growing grace. Amen.

Above all other blessings Oh! God, for ourselves, and our fellow-creatures, we implore Thee to quicken our sense of thy Mercy in the redemption of the World, of the Value of that Holy Religion in which we have been brought up, that we may not, by our own neglect, throw away the salvation thou hast given us, nor be Christians only in name. Hear us Almighty God, for His sake who has redeemed us, and taught us thus to pray. Amen.

JANE AUSTEN

Day 11

'You are mistaken, Elinor,' said [Marianne] warmly, 'in supposing I know very little of Willoughby. I have not known him long indeed, but I am much better acquainted with him, than I am with any other creature in the world, except yourself and mama. It is not time or opportunity that is to determine intimacy;– it is disposition alone. Seven years would be insufficient to make some people acquainted with each other, and seven days are more than enough for others. I should hold myself guilty of greater impropriety in accepting a horse from my brother, than from Willoughby. Of John I know very little, though we have lived together for years; but of Willoughby my judgment has long been formed.'
(*Sense and Sensibility*, chapter 12)

I hold a tender place in my heart for Marianne Dashwood. I suspect it is because she speaks into a section of myself that, now I am deep into my shop-worn fifties, I feel I've lost. Marianne has a youthful capacity for spontaneity and a fullness of sensibility – that sensitivity to the delights and sharpness of the emotions – that I no longer feel is available. As Colonel Brandon says, 'there is something amiable in the prejudices of a young mind'. I have lost such 'prejudices'.

Much as I love Marianne, there is a profound riskiness in her emotion-driven judgements. Her response to her sister Elinor's conviction that she cannot know the object of her love, Willoughby, very well is presented robustly, but it is more than a little bold. It verges on the shrill. Marianne's acquaintance with Willoughby is of recent vintage, the result of an encounter when Marianne injures herself while out walking and Willoughby carries her home. Since that incident their relationship has moved forward rapidly. When Elinor hears from Marianne that Willoughby intends to give her a horse and Marianne is excited about riding every day with him, Elinor is alarmed. The financial implications alone of stabling a horse would be significant for the modest Dashwood household. More troubling still for Elinor is the propriety of Marianne accepting a gift from a man so recently known to her. This is the context for Marianne's speech.

Is Marianne's reading of the situation in any way defensible? Given what we later come to know about Willoughby and the emotional and psychological journey Marianne herself undertakes, we can surely call her naive, if not foolish. Her claim that 'It is not time or opportunity that is to determine intimacy;– it is disposition alone' is surely a recipe for disaster. At the same time, as someone who when young had an excess of sensibility, I 'get' Marianne. Even now, as I write this in fuller knowledge of the risks of excessive sensibility, as well as with better educated senses and emotions (which has become a dangerous tendency to cynicism), I am inclined to over-trust my emotions. The notion of 'love at first sight' is surely absurd. While I don't think that's quite what happens with Marianne, she has an emotional availability that means she is capable of falling in love with great rapidity, perhaps even head over heels. I've done that in my time too, and despite the failures of relationships, I have few regrets. I'm rather in love with being in love. More often than not, my emotion-led passions have not been totally skew-whiff.

I suppose the main bone of contention is Marianne's claim that 'Seven years would be insufficient to make some people acquainted with each other, and seven days are more than enough for others.' It reinforces her claim that intimacy is determined by character and disposition rather than time. She notes that despite living her whole life with her step-brother, she knows him less well than Willoughby. Perhaps it is not Marianne's thinking that is faulty. After all, we can meet people who are so guarded and seemingly locked up, so shy or so shady, that years will not reveal their true selves; there are others whom we meet and within days come to a clear assessment of their trustworthiness or not. Perhaps what is at stake is the extent to which our judgement of people is formed. Discernment and wisdom are crucial. Even then, the mysterious natures of others can lead us to make fools of ourselves.

Thomas Merton said, 'The secret of my full identity is hidden in Him. He alone can make me who I am, or rather who I will be when at last I fully begin to be. But unless I desire this identity and work to find it with Him and in Him, the work will never be done. The way of doing it is a secret I can learn from no one else but Him.'[1] In short, you can only know yourself (and indeed others) more fully insofar as you grow to know God; however, the kicker is that you are called to know a God who eludes our schemes and strategies of control. God is always more than we can imagine. He calls and we are invited to respond. Just as there is mystery at the heart of God and of ourselves, so there is mystery in others and the relationships which emerge between ourselves and others. This is beautiful and hope-filled, but also disconcerting.

Merton suggests that it is imperative that we use our freedom to love, with full responsibility and authenticity. Love here does not resolve into romantic love, though it can include it. Love is that way of being in and with the world that reveals God's desire for healing and reconciliation, justice, mercy and hope. If that is the great song of the universe, romantic love might be seen as a deeply felt, urgent, but minor motif in the wider work: something arresting that, at its best, directs us deeper into wider themes. Lent presents an opportunity to reflect on, interrogate and discern where we and the communities to which we belong align with the Great Work of God. How are we using our freedom to love, with full responsibility and authenticity?

Maybe I should give the final word to Marianne. If, at one level, events prove her a fool (Willoughby fails to be the man she thinks him to be), at another, perhaps, she is right after all. She does know pretty much from the off that their affections are

---

1 Thomas Merton, *New Seeds of Contemplation* (Santa Barbara: Greenwood Publishing Group, 2020), p.16.

potent and life-changing. His failure to be faithful and constant to her does not lie, ultimately, in his lack of passion for her but his lack of character. Though his initial interest in her was of a shallow kind, he does become deeply attached to her. In very many ways, she calls his love for her correctly. His failure (and indeed the sensible judgement against him) lies in how he fails to respect the tender affections of a woman who deserves much more than to be cast off.

Holy God, help me to follow you with hope and love in my heart. Show me sufficient grace that I may follow you this day and be full of good cheer. Amen.

Day 12

Elinor could no longer witness this torrent of unresisted grief in silence.

'Exert yourself, dear Marianne,' she cried, 'if you would not kill yourself and all who love you. Think of your mother; think of her misery while *you* suffer: for her sake you must exert yourself.'

'I cannot, I cannot,' cried Marianne; 'leave me, leave me, if I distress you; leave me, hate me, forget me! but do not torture me so. Oh! how easy for those, who have no sorrow of their own to talk of exertion! Happy, happy Elinor, *you* cannot have an idea of what I suffer.'

'Do you call *me* happy, Marianne? Ah! if you knew! — And can you believe me to be so, while I see you so wretched!'

'Forgive me, forgive me,' throwing her arms round her sister's neck; 'I know you feel for me; I know what a heart you have; but yet you are — you must be happy; Edward loves you — what, oh what, can do away such happiness as that?'

'Many, many circumstances,' said Elinor, solemnly.

'No, no, no,' cried Marianne wildly, 'he loves you, and only you. You *can* have no grief.'

'I can have no pleasure while I see you in this state.'

'And you will never see me otherwise. Mine is a misery which nothing can do away.' (*Sense and Sensibility*, chapter 29)

I marvel at both the differences and the similarities between people. I note also, the older I grow, how very mysterious we are to one another. These kinds of considerations are very close to the surface when I read a passage like that I offer today. Here we have two sisters, raised in the same circumstances and affected by more or less the same challenges, who present quite different characters and personalities. Marianne's emotions are never far from the surface and in this scene, in which she finds out the truth about Willoughby's snub towards her and his intentions to marry another, they are positively torrential. Elinor pleads with her, asking her to calm down; she plays the stereotype of the older sister (responsible, sober, grown-up) to near perfection. We might imagine – rather as Marianne does – that she has little to trouble her, except her pain at the emotional turmoil of her sister. And yet ... quietly, secretly, Elinor is herself what is often called a 'hot mess'. She is in great pain and loneliness as she bears the news that Edward Ferrers is engaged to another.

I love that line: 'torrent of unresisted grief'. Some readers may feel that Marianne's circumstances do not warrant the term 'grief'. Her loss of Willoughby – her first love – has, some might say, the sharpness of the ending of a teenager's first relationship. For anyone who has ever experienced such a thing, it can feel like the end of the world. However, most of us do get over the keen sting of love's first wound soon enough (and Marianne ultimately does too). Is the end of 'first love' truly grief? Does it count as an encounter with the weight of the world? I am inclined to say, 'yes'. The worst thing you have experienced is the worst thing you have experienced. A teenager's grief over the loss of their first love can be heady and painful, especially when they have imbibed the Romantic dream of true love. In the long run other griefs usually supervene, but grief is grief.

As with Marianne and Elinor, each of us will bring our differing personalities to bear as we negotiate grief. Grief is not something we should seek to avoid. It is worth reminding ourselves that the word 'grief' has roots in the concept of weight and burden. Grief makes things heavy and burdensome. It is, then, also a matter for the body. Certainly, we might speak of being grieved in spirit or mind, but grief very much operates through the line of the body. Insofar as it is a burden, grief – for the loss of a loved one, for the death of a relationship, for the death of a way of being in the world – is not readily sloughed off. I guess I'm saying we should not be harsh towards the operatic Marianne, nor the more publicly restrained Elinor; clearly, when someone we love dies we would not fail to recognize the weight of that; nor, however, would I mock someone who continues to feel grief for the loss of important, but not always readily defined, relations and connections. I'm not 'over' Brexit. Nor do I expect I ever shall be. That grief – about who and what this nation was and could be – runs bone-deep.

I love that Wild Goose worship song, 'We will lay our burden down'.[1] It reminds us that in Jesus Christ we can cast our cares on him; it reminds us that Christ's burden is light. This is not because it is weightless and therefore unworthy of grief; rather, it is that as we turn to Christ we move towards the community of love and grace where our burdens, griefs and the costs of a cruel world are held in solidarity and borne together. Today it is worth dwelling on that call to lay our burdens down. We all have them. The reality is that no deep bodily grief is readily thrown off. The work of laying burdens down is a slow work. Rarely is grief thrown to the floor like a backpack at the end of a day's trekking; or if we try, the aftershocks are felt in our bodies as our muscles and viscera adjust to freedom. The good news is that Christ's community of love is available to us. In our solidarity we bear one another's griefs.

Merciful God, you long to meet us in the midst of our griefs and need. Help me be bold, that I may come to you without fear in the assurance of your love in Jesus Christ. Amen.

---

1 https://hymnary.org/text/we_will_lay_our_burden_down

Day 13

'I understand you.—You do not suppose that I have ever felt much.—For four months, Marianne, I have had all this hanging on my mind, without being at liberty to speak of it to a single creature; knowing that it would make you and my mother most unhappy whenever it were explained to you, yet unable to prepare you for it in the least.—It was told me,—it was in a manner forced on me by the very person herself, whose prior engagement ruined all my prospects; and told me, as I thought, with triumph.—This person's suspicions, therefore, I have had to oppose, by endeavouring to appear indifferent where I have been most deeply interested;—and it has not been only once;—I have had her hopes and exultation to listen to again and again.—I have known myself to be divided from Edward for ever, without hearing one circumstance that could make me less desire the connection.—Nothing has proved him unworthy; nor has anything declared him indifferent to me.—I have had to contend against the unkindness of his sister, and the insolence of his mother; and have suffered the punishment of an attachment, without enjoying its advantages.—And all this has been going on at a time, when, as you know too well, it has not been my only unhappiness.—If you can think me capable of ever feeling—surely you may suppose that I have suffered *now*. The composure of mind with which I have brought myself at present to consider the matter, the consolation that I have been willing to admit, have been the effect of constant and painful exertion;—they did not spring up of themselves;—they did not occur to relieve my spirits at first.— No, Marianne.—*Then*, if I had not been bound to silence, perhaps nothing could have kept me entirely—not even what I owed to my dearest friends—from openly shewing that I was *very* unhappy.' (*Sense and Sensibility*, chapter 37)

Human beings have a genius for hiding, dissembling and concealment. In my more cynical moments, I have been tempted to see this as the fundamental mark of our dominance as apex predator. These shadowed and hidden horizons of ourselves make for great plots in detective and spy novels and are the subject of psychoanalytic theory. They generate intrigue and fascination. Sometimes, it is precisely when we are under the most strain or negotiating the highest personal or public stakes that we are most inclined to conceal what's going on in our heads.

As a priest, I've witnessed again and again the wild and wide range of reactions of those under pressure. Consider, for example, the death of a loved one. While some grieve as if they were in a *bel canto* opera, others become even more tightly controlled. It is not that the latter sort of person feels less. Rather, they are negotiating an intense emotional situation in a different way. I've witnessed how, on a personal level, my family reacted to the death of my father on Christmas Day 2021. We all loved him and grieved for him deeply. However, some of us wept copiously; others were quieter and, seemingly, much more controlled. I've learned to judge neither reaction. Character, class, formation and circumstance generate a huge range of responses.

Elinor Dashwood is – in the classic sense of the phrase – a sensible woman. She seeks to keep her sensibility in good regulation. She has received the most personally distressing and disconcerting news: that Edward Ferrers, the man she loves and whom she supposes wishes to become engaged to her, is already attached to Lucy Steele, a fashionable and distressingly shallow young woman. She has learned this news from Lucy herself under conditions of confidentiality. She has negotiated a gamut of emotions from surprise to disbelief and disappointment. She has been left wondering about Edward's judgement. She has held her reactions within herself to such an extent that her own sister Marianne, that queen of unconstrained emotion, and her wider family have no idea of the agonies of emotion Elinor has negotiated. Elinor has carried her emotional baggage around quietly and stoically for four months while Marianne has fallen apart in the aftermath of Willoughby's abandonment. As we later discover, of course, Elinor is a fully alive human being. If she is a little too sensible and needs to become more congruent (well, in touch with her sensibility at least), the famous moment when she 'lets out' her pent-up emotion upon discovering that Edward's engagement to Lucy is off (so memorably performed by Emma Thompson in the 1995 film adaptation) proves the depths of her emotions.

I suspect that a number of elder siblings will recognize the level of responsibility Elinor brings to this scene. My older sister, a first child who often reminds us, her siblings, that she had to be the 'responsible one', certainly would. Elinor balances love for Edward with her love for family. She wants to shield her family from the practical and emotional fallout of the situation she finds herself in. Should she have to? Well, that's moot, I guess. She positions herself as the grown-up in her family, ensuring that the voice of sense is never lost in the emotional soup of the Dashwood home. Equally, by taking up the role of responsibility (under the guise of shielding others from painful knowledge) she shields herself from facing the emotional reality of her situation. She is spared the love and sympathy and tenderness of those nearest to her. This is a horizon of love and mutuality in which she surely needs to grow.

I see no good reason why any of us *should* be required to be like a Marianne rather than an Elinor. It would be absurd to require everyone to have their emotional response or their thoughts on display. Some of us simply are more private than others. Some of us lack language to properly articulate our loves and griefs. Nonetheless, Elinor's situation reminds me to be a little more alert to the way in which those who are seemingly happy may be carrying immense and quiet grief, fear, anxiety and so on. In my priestly ministry, I have noted that men more often than women have a tendency towards living what Thoreau called lives of 'quiet desperation'. I have seen how such behaviours can lead to the bleakest outcome of all: a person taking their own lives.

I note – in my own life – a tendency to put a brave face on personal and public situations. I often struggle to let people in past the façade. This is not the place to attempt some cod self-analysis, but I recognize just how deleterious such a disposition can be to flourishing relationships and my own vocation to grow into the likeness of Christ. So my reflection today resolves into an invitation: to pray for the wisdom to know when to speak and when to be silent; when to hold back and when to find a wise counsellor. Perhaps most of all: to look out for those who, despite appearances to the contrary, are carrying far too much and are at risk of being cut off from the comfort of community, of love and solidarity, and the discovery that we find ourselves more fully when we are in the hands of others. Sometimes, we just need to talk. Sometimes, we need to find communities of character and grace. Sometimes, it is only by giving ourselves over to passion – in the classical sense of allowing ourselves to be in the hands of others – that we grow more like Jesus Christ.

Tender God, Father and Mother of All, you are with us in good times and bad times. Help me to trust in your abiding mercy and dwell in the truth that you always look upon me with eyes of love. Amen.

Day 14

He held out his hand. She could not refuse to give him hers;—he pressed it with affection.

'And you *do* think something better of me than you did?' — said he, letting it fall, and leaning against the mantel-piece as if forgetting he was to go.

Elinor assured him that she did;—that she forgave, pitied, wished him well—was even interested in his happiness—and added some gentle counsel as to the behaviour most likely to promote it. His answer was not very encouraging.

'As to that,' said he, 'I must rub through the world as well as I can. Domestic happiness is out of the question. If, however, I am allowed to think that you and yours feel an interest in my fate and actions, it may be the means—it may put me on my guard—at least, it may be something to live for. Marianne to be sure is lost to me for ever. Were I even by any blessed chance at liberty again—'

Elinor stopped him with a reproof.

'Well,' he replied—'once more good bye. I shall now go away and live in dread of one event.'

'What do you mean?'

'Your sister's marriage.'

'You are very wrong. She can never be more lost to you than she is now.'

'But she will be gained by some one else. And if that some one should be the very he whom, of all others, I could least bear—but I will not stay to rob myself of all your compassionate goodwill, by shewing that where I have most injured I can least forgive. Good bye,—God bless you!'

And with these words, he almost ran out of the room. (*Sense and Sensibility*, chapter 44)

Willoughby is a man about whom we are invited to have strong feelings. He has abandoned Marianne and sought the company of the wealthy Sophia Grey, whom he marries. Even more seriously, we discover from Colonel Brandon that Willoughby behaved infamously to Brandon's ward Eliza Williams: he seduced, impregnated, then abandoned her. His character is, despite his dashing looks, unattractive.

What then are we to make of this encounter between Willoughby and Elinor, taken from late in the novel as Marianne lies ill and perhaps dying? He says the following to express his hopes for the encounter:

> 'I mean if I can, to make you hate me one degree less than you do now. I mean to offer some kind of explanation, some kind of apology, for the past; to open my whole heart to you, and by convincing you, that though I have been always a blockhead, I have not been always a rascal, to obtain something like forgiveness from Ma—from your sister.'

He comes to Elinor, then, aware that he has truly messed up and has barely displayed the kind of civility one would expect of a gentleman. However, his apology is not fulsome. Willoughby reveals to Elinor that his love for Marianne was genuine and that losing her has made him miserable. He elicits Elinor's pity because his choices have made him unhappy, but she is disgusted by the callous way in which he talks of Miss Williams and his own wife. He also reveals that his aunt said she would have forgiven him if he married Miss Williams but that he had refused. After Marianne recovers from her illness and finds out about Willoughby's visit, she realizes that she could never have been happy with Willoughby's immoral, erratic and inconsiderate ways. Willoughby is not a good man. He does love Marianne, however. For Elinor this offers a modest level of mitigation: she comes to pity the miserable bind he finds himself in. Though he loves Marianne abidingly, he is miserably married to another. Perhaps, then, he gets his just deserts for his immoral behaviour (though I'm not sure his wife Sophia deserves her fate to be bound for life to such a man).

As Christians we are called to be people of reconciliation and forgiveness. We are a community shaped around God's abundant offer of reconciliation through his son Jesus Christ. He invites us to turn around – to repent – and face the reality of God and his love. Willoughby's account of himself involves sufficient truth-telling for Elinor to recognize the sincerity of his love for Marianne. However, it is hardly a full confession of his failings and appalling behaviour towards a vulnerable young woman like Eliza Williams. He cannot quite face the reality of immoral and inconsiderate actions. He remains trapped in his shallow self-image. He is worthy of pity but not admiration. He is, simultaneously, a long way off and such a short distance from the honesty and openness that might lead him on the path to redemption.

I cannot, any more than Elinor, commend Willoughby's behaviour and attitude. However, when I think of Willoughby as a human being created in the image of God and called into Christ's likeness, I am reminded how much even those of us who have known conversion and repentance are works in progress. This is not to let Willoughby off the hook; rather, it is to remind us that while Willoughby needs to take responsibility for his vile behaviour, he is not beyond the reach of grace; there is still the possibility of him walking into reality and knowing salvation, though such a walk will be painful for him. This matters as much for each and every one of us. We may not have behaved infamously like him, but we are not righteous. Perhaps you are further along the path of conversion and holiness than I. All I know is that I struggle. Much as I long to know Christ and dwell in him, I am tempted to live in falsehood. I pray daily, as I hope you do, for the transforming grace of God. Without it, we are all lost.

God of Forgiveness, you are more merciful and generous than we dare imagine. When I am tempted to hide from you, grant me grace to turn around to you with penitence in my heart. Amen.

Day 15

'Mrs. Robert Ferrars!'— was repeated by Marianne and her mother in an accent of the utmost amazement;— and though Elinor could not speak, even her eyes were fixed on him with the same impatient wonder. He rose from his seat, and walked to the window, apparently from not knowing what to do; took up a pair of scissors that lay there, and while spoiling both them and their sheath by cutting the latter to pieces as he spoke, said, in a hurried voice,

'Perhaps you do not know – you may not have heard that my brother is lately married to – to the youngest – to Miss Lucy Steele.'

His words were echoed with unspeakable astonishment by all but Elinor, who sat with her head leaning over her work, in a state of such agitation as made her hardly know where she was.

'Yes,' said he, 'they were married last week, and are now at Dawlish.'

Elinor could sit it no longer. She almost ran out of the room, and as soon as the door was closed, burst into tears of joy, which at first she thought would never cease. Edward, who had till then looked any where, rather than at her, saw her hurry away, and perhaps saw – or even heard, her emotion; for immediately afterwards he fell into a reverie, which no remarks, no inquiries, no affectionate address of Mrs. Dashwood could penetrate. (*Sense and Sensibility*, chapter 48)

Elinor and Marianne have received intelligence that 'Mr Ferrers' has married Lucy Steele. They assume this means Edward, rather than his brother Robert. Elinor is – unsurprisingly – hard hit by the news. It signals the end of all her hopes of marriage to her beloved, though she has long thought that her attachment was a forlorn one. Marianne is reduced to hysterics. At which point Edward appears. Astonished though they are that he should visit, Marianne, Elinor and their mother ask after his new wife. Finally, all is revealed: Lucy has married his brother Robert, the new heir to the Ferrers' fortune.

Elinor is so overwhelmed by emotion that she nearly runs from the room. She is overcome with joy and relief. In the classic Ang Lee 1995 adaptation, the scene is handled as an almost uncontrollable explosion of emotion; the usually well-regulated Elinor can no longer control herself. Unconfined sensibility flows up from the very depths of herself. She is in that moment an emotional volcano. And can we be surprised? Part of the sheer joy we feel for Elinor and indeed for Edward is the joy of those who thought hope had been dashed. These are people redeemed into relationship and the full embrace of love.

As I reflect on how *Sense and Sensibility* speaks into the Lenten vocation of Christian soul-examination, I recognize how some of its story shows less sophistication than some of Austen's later novels. As the novel draws to a close, there are questions about how plausible it is that Marianne and Colonel Brandon should get married. Is Marianne sufficiently cured of her excess sensibility? Isn't steady old Brandon just too stolid for Marianne?[1] However, I have no such doubts about Elinor and Edward. There is, I think, something immensely satisfying about the way they are finally united. Elinor, in particular, speaks beautifully into how, in the midst of a managed and controlled hope and profoundly regulated expectation, we can be overwhelmed by joy.

Joy, I think, is not the same as happiness and it is certainly distinct from pleasure. I remember when I was young, before I transitioned and before I became a Christian, how much I sought out pleasure and sensation. There was an emptiness to it. I just wanted to blot out my unhappiness with pleasure. I think I have known, too, a fair share of happiness, that abiding

---

1 The 1995 adaptation handles this question beautifully by giving more space for the relationship between Alan Rickman's Brandon and Kate Winslet's Marianne to breathe.

sense of contentment in relationship with friends and family and, indeed, with self. It is a good place and to be commended. Joy is special, though. It is a kind of breaking-in of grace and wonder and it is not necessarily pleasant or happy. It is a work of God. As C. S. Lewis puts it, 'Joy is the serious business of heaven.' I believe that in the midst of the horror of the cross there is a possibility of joy, the possibility of the Third Day shown forth on Easter morn; joy breaks in and reveals the glory and hope of God. Such joy does not wipe out the cost and horror of the cross. Rather, it dwells in deep attention with and on it. Joy is a terrible and terrific glory and I do hope you have known your share of it, rare though it might be. I think we should all dare to be open to it. Better that than being afraid to live, no matter how costly life is. I hope, too, that we (in our friendships, our loves, and relationships) will have known what Elinor knew:

> But Elinor—how are her feelings to be described?—From the moment of learning that Lucy was married to another, that Edward was free, to the moment of his justifying the hopes which had so instantly followed, she was every thing by turns but tranquil. But when the second moment had passed, when she found every doubt, every solicitude removed, compared her situation with what so lately it had been,—saw him honourably released from his former engagement, saw him instantly profiting by the release, to address herself and declare an affection as tender, as constant as she had ever supposed it to be,—she was oppressed, she was overcome by her own felicity;—and happily disposed as is the human mind to be easily familiarised with any change for the better, it required several hours to give sedateness to her spirits, or any degree of tranquillity to her heart.

God of Joy, in Jesus Christ you show the cost and promise of hope and love. Help us to meet him in our lives this day and become ever more citizens of heaven. Amen.

Day 16

Marianne Dashwood was born to an extraordinary fate. She was born to discover the falsehood of her own opinions, and to counteract, by her conduct, her most favourite maxims. She was born to overcome an affection formed so late in life as at seventeen, and with no sentiment superior to strong esteem and lively friendship, voluntarily to give her hand to another!—and *that* other, a man who had suffered no less than herself under the event of a former attachment, whom, two years before, she had considered too old to be married, — and who still sought the constitutional safeguard of a flannel waistcoat!

But so it was. Instead of falling a sacrifice to an irresistible passion, as once she had fondly flattered herself with expecting,—instead of remaining even for ever with her mother, and finding her only pleasures in retirement and study, as afterwards in her more calm and sober judgment she had determined on,—she found herself at nineteen, submitting to new attachments, entering on new duties, placed in a new home, a wife, the mistress of a family, and the patroness of a village. (*Sense and Sensibility*, chapter 50)

Few who have read *Sense and Sensibility* could doubt the truth and reality of Elinor and Edward's relationship. Marianne and Brandon's, though? There are plenty who feel that Marianne's acceptance of Brandon, indeed her sense of happiness within the relationship, is not properly won. Even though Marianne is scarred by her experiences, is she quite ready, at 19, to marry an admittedly lovely man, but one who – heaven forfend – 'sought the constitutional safeguard of a flannel waistcoat'?

If it is simply the case that *Sense and Sensibility* does not represent the peak of Austen's writing, nonetheless I find Marianne and Brandon's relationship both plausible and quietly satisfying. If Brandon might be characterized as that stock Romance character – the stodgy guy who waits in unrequited love – I admire his steadfastness, kindness and, most of all, his determination not to impose himself on the woman he quietly loves. Marianne, like so many of us who dramatize ourselves, had fantasized a quite different fate to the one she ultimately has. I love that she casts herself as someone destined to a rather sad and wan fate (though personally I find the thought of retirement and study rather appealing) and then discovers that she is called to a busy, public life, exercising patronage and all the responsibilities that go with it. I think Austen is right that so often our lives take turns which take us richly and unexpectedly beyond our fantasies; sometimes we glimpse (as George Herbert puts it) 'heaven in ordinary'. Sometimes the seemingly ordinary and routine reveal more about goodness than a grand dramatic life. Ultimately Brandon and Marianne are a surprisingly well-matched pair. Each has experienced times of trial. Their attachment to one another, which blossoms into mature love, flows not from the wild passions to which Marianne once gave herself, but from the discovery of a moving kind of solidarity and attention. There is a mutual recognition that offers a richer sustenance than raw, burning love. Sense is finally in balance with sensibility.

Love's work does not need to be dramatic or full of wild passion. For some that will be an obvious or banal claim. I suppose that, for me, the realization of the reality that love – human love, divine love – works quietly came late. I had to be tested, changed and shaped by illness and loss. I wanted God in the storm and wind, in the noise of wild music and the drama of life burning bright. And I know God can be found in all of that. However, there is also the space for so much trickery in the pyrotechnics of emotion and show. I am reminded of the story of Elijah on the mountaintop (1 Kings 19). There is earthquake and wind and fire, but God is not in them. It is only in the sound of sheer silence that God can be heard. There is something beautifully ironic about God's self-revelation here. It is an invitation to get beyond the drama and fireworks that seemingly speak of God and come back to the heart of love. Out past drama and out past hurry and spectacle lies the extraordinary, transforming love of God. What might I, you, we, do to seek after that silent speech of God today?

Faithful God, you wait for us with patience and grace. Help me to grow still in your presence, that I may hear your voice clear above the clamouring of my heart and of this world. Amen.

Teach us to understand the sinfulness of our own Hearts, and bring to our knowledge every fault of Temper and every evil Habit in which we have indulged to the discomfort of our fellow-creatures, and the danger of our own Souls. May we now, and on each return of night, consider how the past day has been spent by us, what have been our prevailing Thoughts, Words, and Actions during it, and how far we can acquit ourselves of Evil. Amen.

JANE AUSTEN

Day 17

'I can say nothing for her manner to you as a child; but it was the same with us all, or nearly so. She never knew how to be pleasant to children. But you are now of an age to be treated better; I think she is behaving better already; and when you are her only companion, you *must* be important to her.'

'I can never be important to any one.'

'What is to prevent you?'

'Every thing—My situation—my foolishness and awkwardness.'

'As to your foolishness and awkwardness, my dear Fanny, believe me, you never have a shadow of either, but in using the words so improperly. There is no reason in the world why you should not be important where you are known. You have good sense, and a sweet temper, and I am sure you have a grateful heart, that could never receive kindness without wishing to return it. I do not know any better qualifications for a friend and companion.'

'You are too kind,' said Fanny, colouring at such praise; 'how shall I ever thank you as I ought, for thinking so well of me. Oh! cousin, if I am to go away, I shall remember your goodness to the last moment of my life.' (*Mansfield Park*, chapter 3)

In this early scene from *Mansfield Park*, Fanny is told by her aunt Lady Bertram that she is to be sent away across the park to become the companion of Aunt Norris, her other aunt and the wife of the recently deceased Rector. Fanny does not wish to go, and surely with good reason: Aunt Norris has never shown affection towards her and, as Fanny has grown older, Aunt Norris's cheap asides have only grown more frequent.[1] To

---

1 Indeed, Mrs Norris is a repellent character, who – when Sir Thomas

become her companion would only be the cause of pain. In this
dialogue, the kind Edmund, the only person to really appreciate
Fanny, seeks to persuade her to be reasonable. His kindness
touches her, though he, as much as anyone in the novel, fails to
properly appreciate Fanny's judgement.

For those who think Fanny is a bit of a drip, this passage
supplies evidence. She says she can never be important to anyone, convinced that everything about her – her situation, her
foolishness and awkwardness – will ensure that she will never
be treated with tenderness and fondness. Those of us who want
her to grow a bit of backbone want her to claim a bit of self-
respect. I am intrigued, however, by these extraordinary words
of Edmund's:

> There is no reason in the world why you should not be import-
> ant where you are known. You have good sense, and a sweet
> temper, and I am sure you have a grateful heart, that could
> never receive kindness without wishing to return it. I do not
> know any better qualifications for a friend and companion.

Yes, they startle Fanny and make her blush, giving the reader
a hint of her growing affections for Edmund, but I wonder if
Edmund even begins to understand what he is saying?

'There is no reason in the world why you should not be
important where you are known.' Edmund is fond of Fanny
and wishes to encourage her. He cannot imagine how difficult
it actually will be for Fanny to be with Aunt Norris. He also has
no idea of the hidden truth of his words and how he will need
to grow in order to appreciate them. For *Mansfield Park* is, I
think, in very many ways a working out of that line. Fanny, the

---

heads off to Antigua – leads Mansfield Park ever more astray. In a novel
redolent with discreet critiques of slavery, it is surely no coincidence that
her surname matches that of the infamous Robert Norris, the slaver who
argued vehemently against the abolitionists in parliament. For a superb
analysis of the anti-slavery references and themes in *Mansfield Park* and
of Austen's passionate anti-slavery views, see Paula Byrne, *The Real Jane
Austen* (London: William Collins, 2013 (2014)), pp. 221–3.

meek woman who is constant and steadfast, is undervalued by those around her until she is properly seen and known for who she is. In short, for all Edmund's kindnesses, and the condescension of the likes of her uncle Sir Thomas, she is not appreciated for who she is and how she – in her constancy, love and determination – will effectively reform Mansfield Park. She is, at this point in the novel, neither use nor ornament to Mansfield Park. She is simply not known. It will take the whole novel for Fanny to truly be seen and known.

Along the way, Sir Thomas is exposed as a shallow man who is inclined to see the marriages of his own children in financial terms. Indeed, his whole life has been stained and corrupted by the slavery which, quietly, grubbily, powers his estate; the novel exposes the cupidity of many of those whose lives centre on Mansfield Park. Even Edmund, who is essentially good, is sorely tempted to steer away from his vocation for the sake of materialism and comes – oh so late – to truly see that Fanny is absolutely the right woman for him. It is only at the novel's close – after she has visited her birth family in Portsmouth and returned to Mansfield Park – that Fanny is properly appreciated. It is telling that ultimately it is not Fanny who is condemned to become companion to Aunt Norris, but the disgraced Maria. Aunt Norris and Maria become the matched pair in a kind of earthly purgatory.

'You have good sense, and a sweet temper, and I am sure you have a grateful heart, that could never receive kindness without wishing to return it.' For all her seeming priggishness, I believe that Fanny seeks to live these virtues under not always easy circumstances. She holds fast to them. She does have a grateful heart and is thankful. I think she challenges us on our Christian pilgrimage to model those self-same virtues, often under great pressure. We may not have an Aunt Norris in our lives, but I suspect few of us live in bubbles of applause and congratulation. Life is often pretty tough and it would be understandable if we expressed our irritation and threw a little shade in the direction of those who would undermine us. I've certainly been tempted to do so in the face of the slings and arrows of ministry, and that is OK – because temptation is not sin. Only God is good. However, when we are steadfast in love and character, the world can – albeit quietly and gently – be changed into something more akin to the Kingdom of Heaven.

God of Love, in the midst of this troublous life, grant me a thankful heart. Help me to focus on you and your tenderness this day and always. Amen.

Day 18

'But why are you to be a clergyman? I thought *that* was always the lot of the youngest, where there were many to choose before him.'

'Do you think the church itself never chosen, then?'

'*Never* is a black word. But yes, in the *never* of conversation, which means *not very often*, I do think it. For what is to be done in the church? Men love to distinguish themselves, and in either of the other lines distinction may be gained, but not in the church. A clergyman is nothing.'

'The *nothing* of conversation has its gradations, I hope, as well as the *never*. A clergyman cannot be high in state or fashion. He must not head mobs, or set the ton in dress. But I cannot call that situation nothing which has the charge of all that is of the first importance to mankind, individually or collectively considered, temporally and eternally, which has the guardianship of religion and morals, and consequently of the manners which result from their influence. No one here can call the *office* nothing. If the man who holds it is so, it is by the neglect of his duty, by foregoing its just importance, and stepping out of his place to appear what he ought not to appear.'

'*You* assign greater consequence to the clergyman than one has been used to hear given, or than I can quite comprehend. One does not see much of this influence and importance in society, and how can it be acquired where they are so seldom seen themselves? How can two sermons a week, even supposing them worth hearing, supposing the preacher to have the sense to prefer Blair's to his own, do all that you speak of? govern the conduct and fashion the manners of a large congregation for the rest of the week? One scarcely sees a clergyman out of his pulpit.' (*Mansfield Park*, chapter 9)

This exchange between Mary Crawford and clergyman-to-be Edmund Bertram contains lines and quips which have been deployed in a fair few sermons. I have a vague recollection of this passage being referenced by a bishop in at least one of my licensing services.

As a person of faith and a cleric too, you won't be surprised to read that I am disinclined to take Mary Crawford's part in this conversation. She is, after all, disappointed by Edmund's sense of vocation and is determined to persuade him away from it. However, I think she has something when she says, 'For what is to be done in the church? Men love to distinguish themselves, and in either of the other lines distinction may be gained, but not in the church. A clergyman is nothing.' Even in the early nineteenth century, the potential influence and power of the cleric was not what it had been. For a parish cleric, the best hope was to hold a respectable role within the community with a solid income. The church was not a route to power or distinction. If the cleric had never been a great model for masculine action in the world, to be ordained remained a respectable option for a gentleman. The routes for male distinction in Austen's world lay in being, say, a sea captain like Captain Wentworth in *Persuasion*. Money, fame and distinction could be wrought in fights with the French on the high seas.

For all Edmund's spirited defence of the work and vocation of the parish priest, I'm quietly attracted to Miss Crawford's claim that a cleric is nothing. I wonder, what is so terrible about that? Even admitting Austen's Georgian frame of reference – in which a cleric held a position in society barely recognized today – there is something subversive and challenging in our own age of daring to dwell in the role which is 'nothing'. I like the pun, of course: 'no-thing'. The cleric is a 'parson' or a person, called to invite others into personhood, no matter how lowly or undistinguished (or exalted and distinguished) that may be. More broadly, it is quite something to picture a profession as being about nothing; to show forth Christ as the one who though he was in the form of God, emptied himself and taking the form of a slave takes on human likeness. If the ministry of a priest gathers up all those things that make the church 'The Church' – reconciliation and forgiveness, blessing and so on – then a cleric can show us what it means for all of us, as members of the Royal Priesthood, to be a person, to be no-thing. As I travel deeper into Lent, I certainly think this a worthy matter for self-reflection. I am only too aware of the cost of ministry, especially for clergy and ordinands. It is a ministry too costly and wonderful to be carried in one's own strength alone. It is the work of the whole people of God to cherish and hold one another in our fragility and human need.

However, if all that seems very far from what Austen intends in the quoted passage, or does not quite chime with your longing for a pleasing meditation on her wit, then enjoy also this further exchange between Mary and Edmund in Chapter 11, in which Edmund is again placed on the back foot. Mary thinks it is madness that Edmund should consider it appropriate to 'take holy orders without a living'. She has in mind lazy ministers such as Dr Grant, who like a steady income with little work. I guess we've all encountered such clergy, though I hope far fewer than gossip would sometimes imply: 'A clergyman has nothing to do but be slovenly and selfish—read the newspaper, watch the weather, and quarrel with his wife. His curate does all the work, and the business of his own life is to dine.'

Hopeful God, help me to be open to your generosity this day. May I, through your Son, be a person who builds up rather than tears down, for the sake of your Son. Amen.

Day 19

'This is pretty—very pretty,' said Fanny, looking around her as they were thus sitting together one day; 'every time I come into this shrubbery I am more struck with its growth and beauty. Three years ago, this was nothing but a rough hedgerow along the upper side of the field, never thought of as anything, or capable of becoming anything; and now it is converted into a walk, and it would be difficult to say whether most valuable as a convenience or an ornament; and perhaps, in another three years, we may be forgetting—almost forgetting what it was before. How wonderful, how very wonderful the operations of time, and the changes of the human mind!' And following the latter train of thought, she soon afterwards added: 'If any one faculty of our nature may be called *more* wonderful than the rest, I do think it is memory. There seems something more speakingly incomprehensible in the powers, the failures, the inequalities of memory, than in any other of our intelligences. The memory is sometimes so retentive, so serviceable, so obedient—at others, so bewildered and so weak; and at others again, so tyrannic, so beyond controul!— We are, to be sure, a miracle every way; but our powers of recollecting and of forgetting do seem peculiarly past finding out.'

Miss Crawford, untouched and inattentive, had nothing to say; and Fanny, perceiving it, brought back her own mind to what she thought must interest. (*Mansfield Park*, chapter 22)

Mansfield Park is an extraordinarily sophisticated and subtle novel, in some ways a world away from the clean lines of Austen's early novels. Part of its subtlety lies in its treatment not only of Fanny, but also of a character like Mary Crawford. Mary is no crude anti-heroine. She is caring and charismatic and capable of genuine kindness; if, as we begin to see her through Fanny's eyes, we become ever more aware of her self-regard and materialism, she is no monster.

Mary and Fanny do not have the easiest relationship. Mary is puzzled by Fanny: is she out in society or not? She finds her basically uninteresting. However, in the absence of other young people, she spends time with Fanny. As Mary warms to her, recognizing her uprightness, she is less sure about Mary. Not only does Mary look likely to deflect Fanny's friend (and ultimately husband) Edmund away from priesthood, but reveals herself excessively driven by material things and transactional relationships. Today's excerpt, which takes place in the rectory garden, is striking for the sheer length and eloquence of Fanny's speech. It almost certainly reflects Fanny's youthful reading of *The Idler*, the essays of Samuel Johnson, one of which concerns memory. The concluding thought of that essay, 'the true art of memory is the art of attention' is ironically affirmed in Mary Crawford's lack of response to Fanny's musings.

'How wonderful, how very wonderful the operations of time, and the changes of the human mind!' I've easily lived more than half my life. Living as I do with chronic illness, I am aware of the sheer precariousness of my life. This precariousness tempts me to indulge in at least two unhelpful ways of being in the world. I am tempted to both frenetic activity – to the temptation to try and pack as much into my life as possible – and an excess of nostalgia. While I don't think there is necessarily sin in being busy, I'm unconvinced that rushing around trying to fulfil one's private dreams is a recipe for attention to the richest horizons of love. Equally, the curse of nostalgia lies in how it edits out the mess and complexity of life lived in 'real time'. Things can look marvellous in the rear-view mirror. I am tempted, then, as I grow older, to view the passing of time with anxiety. Nostalgia is a symptom of just such an anxiety, I fear. It makes my heart ache. Maybe I will be like Hugh Moreland in Anthony Powell's *A Dance To The Music of Time*: I shall be killed by nostalgia.

To attempt to reflect on capital 'T' time is likely to induce vertigo. Nonetheless, there is, as Fanny suggests, something marvellous about time and what its passage makes available. To treat well with time requires trust. Her reflections on the changes in the rectory garden are good ones, no worse for being conventional. I'm no gardener, but surely hope and trust are required for the full flourishing of a garden: often one does not live long enough to see a tree come to its full flowering. There is hope in trusting in the workings out of time. God's time, however, is on another level. It is – to borrow Fanny's word – genuinely *marvellous*. God's time lingers, disturbs and generates marvel because it begins precisely where we don't expect: the starting point is Resurrection. God makes an extraordinary invitation to accept that the truest reading of time and hope and promise comes when we locate ourselves in the realm of Resurrection or Third Day. The telling point of the adventure is the news shown on the Third Day. God's story, in which we are invited to locate our stories, is a reading backwards and forwards in dynamic relationship. In Resurrection we reach back into Passion; in Passion we reach forward into Resurrection. Third Day is First Day; First Day is Third Day. The invitation is to dare to live in this promise and wonder and inhabit a world turned upside down.

'If any one faculty of our nature may be called more wonderful than the rest, I do think it is memory.' Fanny's reflections, filtered through the prism of Samuel Johnson, rightly draw attention to the curious nature of memory. Memory can be both unstable and pin-sharp. Memories have the capacity to comfort as well as torment us. Perhaps the appeal of nostalgia is that it represents the realm where memory (even false or edited memory) is sovereign. Memory and memories tell us and others so much about ourselves. I have witnessed the erosion of memory due to dementia too often to underestimate its significance at a personal level. Memory at the corporate level requires rehearsal too if we, as a species or as communities, are to resist the sins represented by ethical hell-sites like the Shoah.

Memory can also be a work of letting go. It can be shaped through trust and a resistance to the panic-measures generated by a world that seems constructed to generate anxiety. This kind of memory is the memory and remembrance inscribed in the Eucharist. This memory is resilient to our own lapses of memory as well as the cruel and horrifying erasure of individual memory produced by disease. It is held at the level of the Body of Christ. It is held in the memory of the Living God. We can participate in this remembering and remembrance whether we are young or old, memory-full or memory-absent, queer or straight, and so on and so forth. This is radical memory which holds us and sets us free from our understandable and specific anxieties. In it we dwell in God's time and reality. In Luke 12.35, Jesus asks, 'And can any of you by worrying add a single hour to your span of life?' No. However, in the abundant and divine grace of God's memory we find the fullness of life and liberation from fear. It is marvellous. It is the place we are called to dwell.

God of All, help me to let go of all that would separate me from you today. May I and all those whom I love find our lives in you. Amen.

Day 20

'The sweets of housekeeping in a country village!' said Miss Crawford archly. 'Commend me to the nurseryman and the poulterer.'

'My dear child, commend Dr. Grant to the deanery of Westminster or St. Paul's, and I should be as glad of your nurseryman and poulterer as you could be. But we have no such people in Mansfield. What would you have me do?'

'Oh! you can do nothing but what you do already: be plagued very often, and never lose your temper.'

'Thank you; but there is no escaping these little vexations, Mary, live where we may; and when you are settled in town and I come to see you, I dare say I shall find you with yours, in spite of the nurseryman and the poulterer, perhaps on their very account. Their remoteness and unpunctuality, or their exorbitant charges and frauds, will be drawing forth bitter lamentations.'

'I mean to be too rich to lament or to feel anything of the sort. A large income is the best recipe for happiness I ever heard of. It certainly may secure all the myrtle and turkey part of it.'

'You intend to be very rich?' said Edmund, with a look which, to Fanny's eye, had a great deal of serious meaning.

'To be sure. Do not you? Do not we all?' (*Mansfield Park*, chapter 22)

A few years ago I watched the Mark Gatiss/Steven Moffat adaptation of *Dracula*. I gave it a 'D Minus', though it had some insightful moments. One of those moments happens early in the final episode. Dracula awakes from a century-long imprisonment to find himself in the twenty-first century. He enters the home of someone who, in our society, is financially poor. Yet, as the ancient Dracula takes in the surroundings – the large number of possessions, the warmth and comfort, the fact that light is available at the flick of a switch – he marvels. When the person who lives in the house tells Dracula she is poor he doesn't believe her. He notes that the house has amenities which would have outmatched a king's in his day. He says that, in his century, a person would not leave their home if they had such marvels.

'A large income is the best recipe for happiness I ever heard of.' I wonder if you read Mary Crawford's potentially taste-less sentence somewhat differently when it is contextualized in a Georgian society in which – beneath the veneer of gentility and the comforts found at its apex – life was often brief and exhausting, especially for women. In any context in which com-fort is for the few and not for the many, isn't Mary's statement basically honest? It is worth noting that, as Britain industrial-ized in the early nineteenth century, agricultural workers and their families fled to towns like Manchester. This was not for their own health. They were greeted by squalor. They went in search of good wages and the prospect of a better standard of living. There was not a huge flight back to the countryside, a context itself which was shifting fast and increasingly impacted by modern farming methods.

My sister researched our family history a few years ago; we were the 'below stairs' sort of people one finds in Jo Baker's *Longbourn*. If I were living in Mary Crawford's time, I should be unsentimental: I should want to be wealthy. I should, at least, want to have a large enough income that I could act as if wanting a large income was distasteful.[1] Jesus is right: you cannot serve Mammon and God, but in a ruthlessly divided world having sufficient money to live well is not to be mocked. In our own time, in which more and more people are falling into poverty, I think none of us should underestimate the attraction of wealth. There is a reason so many go in search of it.

---

[1] This is basically Edmund's position when he jokes that Mary only need fix on the amount she needs and she shall have it. He intends 'only not to be poor'.

There is a modern phrase that might help us navigate our reactions to today's passage: 'You said the quiet part out loud.' It is typically used in the context of public policy and political announcements.[2] Thus, a government minister might say they wish to ensure that their constituents have greater security and safety. This is not an unreasonable desire. However, the 'quiet part' is the aspect of such a policy that the politician would not wish to say for fear of alienating the majority of voters (for example, that in order to achieve this end they will scapegoat an outsider group). In a political culture where brazenness has become standard, public figures have increasingly said the quiet part out loud. They have exposed their ulterior motives. I don't think Mary Crawford's statement has an ulterior motive. However, her bold statement about the importance of significant wealth is what many of us might call tasteless; it is not the sort of thing you might expect someone of good manners to say 'out loud'. It is something which is better kept to yourself. Certainly, I think that Edmund Bertram is shocked by Mary's brazenness. He glimpses her tendency to commodify life: love is ultimately about conquest and power. Its analogue is power exercised via wealth.

It is easy to act as if wealth does not matter. As a Christian, I do not want money to regulate and order my life and priorities. However, as someone who once lived on disability benefits and, certainly in my very early life, knew what it was to grow up without money, it is distasteful to pretend that money is not something desirable. Perhaps Mary Crawford's candour is the best policy. Or perhaps the better path – even in the midst of the financial cruelties of our own time – is to seek to properly order our priorities. It would be too crass to say that those of us who grew up without wealth had better consolations, things like friendship or family and so on. However, I have to say I am grateful that I grew up in a context where money was very far from everything. In my view, the warmth of loving relationship knocks wealth into a cocked hat.

---

2 It was first used in *The Simpsons* in 1995.

I want, this Lent, to come back to those moving words of St Paul: 'I regard everything as loss because of the surpassing value of knowing Christ Jesus my Lord.' Paul is speaking about letting go of the privileges he had as one who grew up as part of God's covenant. Increasingly, I feel challenged to interrogate the privileges of my own life; I want to place them in the context of the surpassing value of knowing Jesus. I know that can sound horrifyingly pious, and it probably is pious; however, it is also a point of disruption and breakage in my valuing of things. By centring on the love and embrace of Christ, we might, just might, begin to locate our values and priorities in him. We might be able to live more simply and not be mesmerized by fear or driven by money. I know that when I stay close to Jesus I fight harder for the transformation of the world so that everyone is fed and has enough money on which to live. Christ's priorities are the priorities that lead to the fullness of life.

Fearless God, when we are tempted to fall away from your ways, surround us with your encouragement and love. Help me to stay close to Jesus. Amen.

Day 21

'Ha!' she cried, with instant animation, 'am I here again? The East room! ... The scene we were rehearsing was so very remarkable! The subject of it so very—very—what shall I say? He was to be describing and recommending matrimony to me ... I suppose no time can ever wear out the impression I have of his looks and voice as he said those words. It was curious, very curious, that we should have such a scene to play! If I had the power of recalling any one week of my existence, it should be that week—that acting week. Say what you would, Fanny, it should be *that*; for I never knew such exquisite happiness in any other. His sturdy spirit to bend as it did! Oh! it was sweet beyond expression. But alas, that very evening destroyed it all. That very evening brought your most unwelcome uncle. Poor Sir Thomas, who was glad to see you? Yet, Fanny, do not imagine I would now speak disrespectfully of Sir Thomas, though I certainly did hate him for many a week. No, I do him justice now. He is just what the head of such a family should be. Nay, in sober sadness, I believe I now love you all.' ...

And embracing her very affectionately, 'Good, gentle Fanny! when I think of this being the last time of seeing you for I do not know how long, I feel it quite impossible to do anything but love you.'

Fanny was affected. She had not foreseen anything of this, and her feelings could seldom withstand the melancholy influence of the word 'last'. She cried as if she had loved Miss Crawford more than she possibly could; and Miss Crawford, yet further softened by the sight of such emotion, hung about her with fondness, and said, 'I hate to leave you. I shall see no one half so amiable where I am going. Who says we shall not be sisters? I know we shall. I feel that we are born to be connected; and those tears convince me that you feel it too, dear Fanny.'

Fanny roused herself, and replying only in part, said, 'But you are only going from one set of friends to another. You are going to a very particular friend.' ...

After this speech the two girls sat many minutes silent, each thoughtful; Fanny meditating on the different sorts of friendship in the world, Mary on something of less philosophic tendency. (*Mansfield Park*, chapter 36)

The friendship between Mary and Fanny has emerged slowly and, despite the display of emotion in this scene, remains equivocal. Mary has come to appreciate Fanny's steadiness and constancy (and availability?), but she remains, nonetheless, hardly the kind of fashionable friend Mary truly desires, despite her evident sincerity in this scene. For Fanny, too, this scene reveals the limits of her friendship with Mary. She has become attached to Mary, but the East Room is a site of pain for Fanny: it is where, as Fanny acted as prompter, Edmund and Mary rehearsed the roles of lovers in the proposed play. For Mary the remembrance of this rehearsal ('the acting week') may be happy, but for Fanny it is painful.

Austen mainlines here the messiness and richness of friendship. Mary is no simple cipher for selfishness or wickedness; she is a real human being, absolutely capable of consistent love and devotion. She reveals the extent to which some human beings are a curious combination of the substantial and insubstantial. Mary adored the acting week, not least because it provided conditions for her and Edmund to use surrogate words to express their emerging love; the realm of the drama allowed the young people, ordinarily restricted by good order and form, to engage in a kind of risky play. Acting week allowed the young people to enter the make-believe of childhood again, with the added stakes of edgy adult intimacy. Part of the 'social upheaval' modelled by the genteel young people's proposal to put on a play lies in the way it allows them to try on alternative masks and identities. Friendship, love, hate and so on can be simulated, tested out and then discarded. Fanny's refusal to act – 'No, indeed I cannot act' – has even been taken by the critic

Nina Auerbach as a token of her strangeness: that she is a kind of literary, queer monster.

For Fanny, the play week is painful for various reasons: it reveals to her how ill-fit she is for the sophisticated games of adult life, as well as revealing that the man she loves, Edmund, may be drawn away from good sense by Mary. Fanny's character is not made for make-believe. She has struggled to find her place in the world of Mansfield Park and she lacks the position and confidence to mess about with it or – as we might say in our own context – fake it. She has – for modern tastes – a disconcerting lack of trust in fakery. The things that matter – friendship, love, family, good human relationships – have a substance that is not to be messed about with. If, at this stage of the novel, she retains a certain naivety about the nature of relationships, not least about her birth family, there is a steadfastness in Fanny that no doubt partly reflects her disrupted childhood.

'Fanny meditated on the different sorts of friendship in the world.' It doesn't take a genius to understand why Fanny's steadfastness and loyalty to substantial and substantive friendships across time can appear to a reader as priggish or odd. Not unreasonably, during the 'play week' you might wish to shout, 'Oh come on, Fanny, just let go and have some fun. You're a young woman, not a maiden aunt clutching at your pearls.' As a lover of all things theatre, that is certainly my instinctive reaction.[1] Nonetheless, Fanny reminds us that the judgements of Austen's characters (and Austen herself) do not readily translate to an age like ours that prioritizes charm and the other techniques of the social chameleon.[2] To a certain extent Mary Crawford has the capacity to take on and slew off

---

1 I am inclined to agree with my friend Mads Davies who, when wondering what the contemporary equivalent of the shock created by 'Play Week' would be, suggests that we might be outraged by people using fake personas on social media.

2 Though it is important to note that Austen, herself, adored the theatre. She took part in Austen family 'productions' from an early age and loved to attend professional performances.

friends according to context and circumstance. She is socially accomplished. Friendship is both real – she is not a psychopathic monster for whom others are merely characters in her own drama – and profoundly adaptive. Constancy is not an abiding virtue in her friendships.

Aristotle's famous analysis of friendship in the *Nichomachean Ethics* proposes three classic forms of friendship: that of utility, that of pleasure and that of virtue. Of these, the latter presents the ultimate form of friendship: it is that which both models and facilitates the formation of virtue and the growth of character. Perhaps most of our friendships are like those of Mary Crawford: grounded in utility (friendships of (mutual) convenience where the tenor is what one can gain from them) or pleasure (the rather self-centred, but nonetheless attractive pursuit of fun and sensation). Virtuous friendship is a rare thing, and requires desiring the best for the other, as well as a preparedness to let go of overweening self-interest. Jesus, of course, is serious about friendship. In John's Gospel (15.15), he says, 'I do not call you servants any longer, because the servant does not know what the master is doing; but I have called you friends, because I have made known to you everything that I have heard from my Father.' In Christ, we are invited into the fullness of friendship with the Living God. This is a relationship of mutual recognition. As we come to recognize Jesus Christ in others, and in our friendships and intimate relationships, we are set free to genuinely desire the full flourishing of others. Jesus says, 'No one has greater love than this, that they lay down their life for their friends' (John 15.13). Jesus reveals the definitive shape of grace in his self-offering for the sake of the world; he invites those who would follow him to shape their way of being in the world after his Way.

We, as much as Fanny, Edmund or Mary, are made in and for relationship. Lent is not merely an opportunity to seek to interrogate our relationship with ourselves or with God; it offers space to reflect hopefully and deeply on our fruitful friendships and relationships and how we might be better friends and relations. I am only too aware of my own failures in relationships, in friendships, and in desiring the best for family. I can't be alone in this. At this point in my journey, I suspect I'm not going to change radically. However, I can shift by degrees. As I am attentive to, and seek to be formed in, the virtuous love of Christ who calls me out of myself and into grace, I change. The sacrificial love of Christ can be part of our human relationships. We too can be steadfast in our longing for the full flourishing of our friends and relations and act accordingly.

Gracious God, you make us for relationship with you and one another. Help me this day to take my place in your community of love. Amen.

Day 22

Scarcely had [Edmund] done regretting Mary Crawford, and observing to Fanny how impossible it was that he should ever meet with such another woman, before it began to strike him whether a very different kind of woman might not do just as well—or a great deal better, whether Fanny herself were not growing as dear, as important to him in all her smiles and all her ways, as Mary Crawford had ever been; and whether it might not be a possible, an hopeful undertaking to persuade her that her warm and sisterly regard for him would be foundation enough for wedded love …

With such a regard for her, indeed, as his had long been, a regard founded on the most endearing claims of innocence and helplessness, and completed by every recommendation of growing worth, what could be more natural than the change? Loving, guiding, protecting her, as he had been doing ever since her being ten years old, her mind in so great a degree formed by his care, and her comfort depending on his kindness, an object to him of such close and peculiar interest, dearer by all his own importance with her than any one else at Mansfield, what was there now to add, but that he should learn to prefer soft light eyes to sparkling dark ones.—And being always with her, and always talking confidentially, and his feelings exactly in that favourable state which a recent disappointment gives, those soft light eyes could not be very long in obtaining the pre-eminence.

Having once set out, and felt that he had done so, on this road to happiness, there was nothing on the side of prudence to stop him or make his progress slow; no doubts of her deserving, no fears of opposition of taste, no need of drawing new hopes of happiness from dissimilarity of temper. Her mind, disposition, opinions, and habits wanted no half-concealment, no self-deception on the present, no reliance on future improvement. Even in the midst of his late infatuation, he had acknowledged Fanny's mental superiority. What must be his sense of it now, therefore? She was of course only too good for him; but as nobody minds having what is too good for them, he was very steadily earnest in the pursuit of the blessing, and it was not possible that encouragement from her should be long wanting. Timid, anxious, doubting as she was, it was still impossible that such tenderness as hers should not, at times, hold out the strongest hope of success, though it remained for a later period to tell him the whole delightful and astonishing truth. His happiness in knowing himself to have been so long the beloved of such a heart, must have been great enough to warrant any strength of language in which he could clothe it to her or to himself; it must have been a delightful happiness. But there was happiness elsewhere which no description can reach. Let no one presume to give the feelings of a young woman on receiving the assurance of that affection of which she has scarcely allowed herself to entertain a hope. (*Mansfield Park*, chapter 48)

When we compare this scene with the denouements of *Pride and Prejudice*, *Sense and Sensibility* or even *Emma*, it is not difficult to understand why the more romantic among us might find ourselves a little disappointed. For those who live for the grand ending, this low-key offering is a fail. Furthermore, from a feminist point of view, these paragraphs might become a source of significant irritation. They imply that Fanny has to deal with Edmund's blathering on at her about how much he misses Miss Crawford; she then – effectively – has to deal with the fact that while he comes to appreciate her as equal, if not superior, to his lost love, she is seen as in some ways second-best. Certainly, the masterful use of indirect speech here gives us insight into Edmund's thought processes. They are not, at every point, hugely appealing, not least the enumeration of the ways in which Fanny would be most suitable as a wife. I suspect that many of us, in Fanny's position, would be tempted to give

Edmund an entirely unladylike raised finger and tell him to jog on.

Of course, I'm not sure such a reading of the text is fair or sufficiently nuanced. The third paragraph of this excerpt is, in my view, a masterpiece, both in composition and insight into the emergence of real human love. The paragraph manages to frame two perspectives – that of Edmund and that of Fanny – in fresh, moving prose; crucially, it holds a deep, awesome passion in a way that feels earthed rather than breathless or gushy. In this passage we encounter love refracted through the prism of real lives known in depth over time. It captures how much of love is about discernment and steadfast attention and hope (rather than 'mic-drop' emotional moments). Edmund's journey into the love that will change him over a lifetime is about veils being lifted; it is about an education in character and vision. For Fanny, we hear vindication of her steadfastness; we also hear of love as the persistence of hope. The more time I spend with the denouement the more deeply I am moved.

I suspect that my thoughts regarding steadfast hope and the importance of the education of the emotions for the formation of character sound horribly old-fashioned. I guess I sound like a fuddy-duddy. So be it. The philosopher Alasdair MacIntyre suggests that Fanny's vindication (and indeed the arc of *Mansfield Park* itself) makes Austen 'the last great effective imaginative voice' of virtue ethics. Fanny's 'lack of charm is crucial to Jane Austen's intentions' because 'charm is the characteristic modern quality which those who lack or simulate the virtues use to get by'.[1] Fanny's path presents a 'middle way' between the ceaseless motion of Mary Crawford and the indolence of Mrs Norris. In a readily distracted age, such as ours, Fanny's very constancy is difficult to spot for the virtue it is. Indeed, Edmund himself takes an age to spot it. While he has sufficient sense and character to know Fanny's goodness from their earliest encounter, it is only when the charm of Mary is seen

---

1 Alasdair MacIntyre, *After Virtue: A Study in Moral Theory*, 2nd edn (London: Duckworth, 1985), p. 242.

through that he can truly enter the truth. For him to become the person he is truly called to be, he must be further educated through the truth and goodness of the one substantial person in *Mansfield Park*: Fanny Price. She may appear a milksop to us, but she is the real deal.

I, like many, have too often relied on charm to survive and thrive in our post-modern world. I am a product of this present age. I see how close I and many of my contemporaries are to ghoulish figures, some of whom have held high political office or are confidence tricksters, who use charm as a substitute for character. Fanny Price scares the life out of me. Nonetheless I see, all too readily, how much I – as a person of faith – am called to locate my life in a community of character and grace. I am caught up in an ongoing work of conversion to Jesus Christ; I am invited to locate my life in him and called into virtue. If this is a costly path it is also the path of hope and joy. I suspect that part of my fear of virtue is grounded in a fear of being read as priggish or dull or pious. The real working-out of virtue, however, does not produce superciliousness or a poverty of joy or boldness. You only need to cursorily inspect the life of Jesus to appreciate that.

I am convinced that one sound and substantive way of understanding 'love' is as 'hope persevering'. There is a toughness and steadfastness in such a way of being in the world. It is not to be resolved into charm or fleeting emotion. It is a work of character. Fanny Price is not perfect. However, it is quite a disruptive thought to consider how much we should aspire to be more like her. She shows us more about hope persevering than dozens of other fictional heroes of which we're supposed to be in awe. She invites us to reconsider our reference points for love, hope and practical holiness. Dare I say it, she points towards Christ.

Jesus Christ, you are my Peace, world without end. Thank you for your faithful and sacrificial love. Grant me a place at your Table and help me to have the trust to let you serve. Amen.

Pardon oh God! whatever thou has seen amiss in us, and give us a stronger desire of resisting every evil inclination and weakening every habit of sin. Thou knowest the infirmity of our nature, and the temptations which surround us. Be thou merciful, oh heavenly Father! to creatures so formed and situated. We bless thee for every comfort of our past and present existence, for our health of body and of mind and for every other source of happiness which thou hast bountifully bestowed on us. Amen.

JANE AUSTEN

Day 23

Emma Woodhouse, handsome, clever, and rich, with a comfortable home and happy disposition, seemed to unite some of the best blessings of existence; and had lived nearly twenty-one years in the world with very little to distress or vex her.

She was the youngest of the two daughters of a most affectionate, indulgent father; and had, in consequence of her sister's marriage, been mistress of his house from a very early period. Her mother had died too long ago for her to have more than an indistinct remembrance of her caresses; and her place had been supplied by an excellent woman as governess, who had fallen little short of a mother in affection.

Sixteen years had Miss Taylor been in Mr. Woodhouse's family, less as a governess than a friend, very fond of both daughters, but particularly of Emma. Between them it was more the intimacy of sisters. Even before Miss Taylor had ceased to hold the nominal office of governess, the mildness of her temper had hardly allowed her to impose any restraint; and the shadow of authority being now long passed away, they had been living together as friend and friend very mutually attached, and Emma doing just what she liked; highly esteeming Miss Taylor's judgment, but directed chiefly by her own.

The real evils, indeed, of Emma's situation were the power of having rather too much her own way, and a disposition to think a little too well of herself; these were the disadvantages which threatened alloy to her many enjoyments. The danger, however, was at present so unperceived, that they did not by any means rank as misfortunes with her. (*Emma*, chapter 1)

These sentences were my first encounter with Jane Austen. I can't read them now without a smile. Back in 1986, I marvelled only at their seeming banality. Who cares, I then thought, if this woman has all the advantages on earth? Why should I care about her version of 'first world problems'? What has this to tell me?

Part of the pleasure of this passage lies in the way it subtly yields two images of Emma: one that flatters her privilege and one that quietly undercuts it. She *is* handsome, clever and rich, with a comfortable home and a happy disposition. However, as the novel unfolds, we discover that this is as much a complacent self-assessment as a statement of fact. We are invited to enjoy her advantages and sureties as much as she does herself. Yet running alongside this picture is another one which is more critical, indicating the trip-hazards Emma's complacency will throw in her way: we are told that she has grown to adulthood with little to vex or distress her. Why is this? Certainly, she knows the privileges of middle-class gentility, but more importantly she has ruled her little roost. Her temper and disposition have not been framed by education or good parental role models. Emma's father – whom we discover is a deeply complacent and selfish valetudinarian masquerading as a good-hearted old man – is indulgent only insofar as it suits his own comfort; her sister has married, thereby escaping the family home; her compliant governess, Miss Taylor (who becomes Mrs Weston), had absolutely no authority or control. Indeed, 'the mildness of her temper had hardly allowed her to impose any restraint'.

In short, much as Emma is presented as deeply blessed indeed, she is also spoilt. As we read in the last paragraph of this excerpt, Emma is so wrapped up in herself and her good fortune that she cannot begin to appreciate the threat this poses to others and herself. Her overinflated sense of self and position could generate real harm. It will take a good many misadventures – not least her horribly misjudged behaviour towards Harriet Smith – as well as the presence of consistent, loving wisdom, offered by the truthful and steadfast Mr Knightley, for her to truly grow up and find her way.

Why do we care for Emma and her fate? Doesn't Emma just come across as some spoilt rich kid who has too much time and money, lacking the guidance of a wise grown-up? For all her gentility, she's gone a bit rogue. Indeed, the 1995 movie *Clue-less*, which is loosely based on *Emma*, turns Emma into Cher, a popular and rich Beverley Hills schoolgirl.[1] Maybe I'm also hyper-alert to the question of Emma's likeability because I grew up as an over-indulged child, too readily let off responsibility. I was spoilt. I had an over-inflated sense of my own importance. It took me years to begin to get a better perspective on why the world didn't revolve around me.

Perhaps one answer to the question why we care for Emma's fate lies in the fact that, for all her bossiness and interfering, she's 'not all that'. For all that she might like to act the great lady, she is only notable in her small community. She is no lady of national statue. She is a woman respected in her parish. She might hold privilege, but it's local privilege. For me, that softens my heart towards Emma. She becomes a recognizable person: of parochial clout, a bit pretentious, but young, naive and actually quite fragile. The older I grow, the more I find youth moving; not because I miss it, but because the young are so vulnerable. They seem so defenceless. Equally, while she is old enough to be responsible for her actions, she is not to blame for the fact that she is the product of a less than rounded upbringing. The hope in her situation lies in her capacity to grow and see herself and her interfering actions for what they are: mistakes and fantasies that could have dreadful implications for vulnerable people like Harriet as well as for herself. The ironic pleasure of the novel lies, in part, in the length of time it takes for the bright and essentially good-hearted Emma to realize the nature of reality, and the love and goodness embedded in them.

The great Jesuit writer Gerry Hughes once claimed that God is in the facts, and therefore the facts must be kind. I've wrestled with that statement on and off for decades. Certainly, as is commonly claimed in politics, facts are our friends: they enable us to form the basis for solid judgements and actions. As Emma shows, however, facts do tend to get refracted through

---

1 It has to be said that *Clueless* is a minor classic in which Silverstone's Cher goes on a very satisfying redemptive arc.

the lens of our own bias. I suspect some of us never quite realize just how much our perspective skews reality. It is a matter for rejoicing that Emma comes to a place of clarity as rapidly as she does. Still, I want to come back to the idea that God is in the facts. Of that I have no doubt. Does that make the facts kind? As someone who has witnessed a fair share of injustice as well lived through a good portion of personal pain and suffering, I want to add: 'and sometimes they're unkind'. Perhaps a fuller unpacking of the classic line is 'God is in the facts and in the promise ... the promise cannot be erased by the facts, but grows out of and in the midst of them'. We are called to stay with reality and get to know it better. That's a vocation worth having. I think it is ultimately the vocation Emma begins to discern as she steps out in faith and love with Mr Knightley. Reality holds us to account, but it also exposes us to actual living human beings with desires and hopes; as we treat with reality they grow less like cardboard cut-outs or walk on parts in our drama. Lent is an invitation to step deeper into *the* drama; to dare to see love and hope breaking through and present in the midst of the facts of the world.

God of Abundant Grace, show me more of your world of love and truth this day. When I am tempted to run away in fear, help me to stay, serve, and trust. Amen.

Day 24

She was not struck by any thing remarkably clever in Miss Smith's conversation, but she found her altogether very engaging—not inconveniently shy, not unwilling to talk—and yet so far from pushing, shewing so proper and becoming a deference, seeming so pleasantly grateful for being admitted to Hartfield, and so artlessly impressed by the appearance of every thing in so superior a style to what she had been used to, that she must have good sense, and deserve encouragement. Encouragement should be given. Those soft blue eyes, and all those natural graces, should not be wasted on the inferior society of Highbury and its connexions. The acquaintance she had already formed were unworthy of her. The friends from whom she had just parted, though very good sort of people, must be doing her harm. They were a family of the name of Martin, whom Emma well knew by character, as renting a large farm of Mr. Knightley, and residing in the parish of Donwell—very creditably, she believed—she knew Mr. Knightley thought highly of them—but they must be coarse and unpolished, and very unfit to be the intimates of a girl who wanted only a little more knowledge and elegance to be quite perfect. *She* would notice her; she would improve her; she would detach her from her bad acquaintance, and introduce her into good society; she would form her opinions and her manners. It would be an interesting, and certainly a very kind undertaking; highly becoming her own situation in life, her leisure, and powers. (*Emma*, chapter 3)

Do you believe in the goodness of social mobility? As someone who has travelled across and through real, if not always readily defined, class lines, I'm inclined to say 'yes'. I was surprised, therefore, when a friend from a much more privileged background to mine proclaimed that most people would be much happier if they did not move outside the sphere in which they'd been born. While I don't think this person was channelling Lady Catherine de Bourgh, he held a broadly High Tory perspective in which the goodness of tradition and class were to be presumed; he allowed that nature might throw up 'natural aristocrats' from time to time, but that the vast majority of people should 'stay in their lane'.

There is clearly a world of difference between a self-motivated person seeking improvement via education or taking advantage of the available social opportunities and someone who is made a *Pygmalion* project by another person. Harriet Smith is no Becky Sharp; equally, Emma Woodhouse's treatment of Harriet is, at best, misguided and, at worst, an example of treating a simple-hearted and trusting person as a plaything or doll. The passage we read today suggests, I think, that Emma is not malicious. Rather, she is guilty of something of which we can all be guilty: seeing in another what we want to see. In short, of projecting on to another person an image that suits us and perhaps, even, reflects a little of what we want to see in ourselves. Harriet clearly is a sweet young woman with few prospects, but Emma takes her artlessness and transforms it into a kind of simple virtue that only needs to be shaped by a superior person – herself! Rather than read Harriet as a little in awe of her elegance and pleased to be noticed by an important person in the neighbourhood, Emma reads this deference as a token of goodness that just needs a bit of adjustment in order for Harriet to take her place in a higher sphere of life.

The more I've read *Emma* the more I've grown to feel for Harriet. This passage mentions Mr Martin, the yeoman farmer much approved of by Knightley. The truth is that Martin was not of so distinctly a lower class as Emma thinks. He is a good man of solid position in his community. The simple fact that he is held in such high esteem by the finest gentleman in the neighbourhood should signal to Emma that he is a suitable match for a genteel, if unheralded, young woman like Harriet. Due to Emma's interference, however, rather than Martin and

Harriet marrying early in the novel, they almost don't marry at all. Harriet really is not treated with respect and proper kindness by Emma. I guess Emma's behaviour makes for a good novel. The fact that Emma is forced to recognize her love for Knightley only when she becomes anxious that he likes Harriet is satisfying. However, at a human level, I want Harriet to find happiness sooner rather than later.

Perhaps I should not be too harsh on Emma. She is young and, frankly, though I am much older than her I'm not sure I am any more immune to the sins of projection and seeing in others what I want to see. Perhaps we all see each other more often than not through a mirror dimly. Insofar as that is the case, it invites us to model a prudent modesty in our assessments of the actions of others. That is risky, of course. There are some out there who are, frankly, nothing more than bounders, chancers and sociopaths who will exploit our trust and generosity for their own purposes. The development of a certain level of good judgement is wise. However, a searching self-awareness of one's own capacity for projection and bias, aligned to a thoughtful appreciation of the fragilities of others, will certainly help us negotiate the temptation to those most modern sins, cynicism and othering. In this life we are condemned to see through a mirror dimly; only as we participate more fully in the reality of God do we begin to see 'face to face', with all the clarity that brings.

Faithful God, in your goodness you do not give up on us. Help us not to give up on you. Help us to stand with you in your hour of need. Amen.

Day 25

The first error and the worst lay at her door. It was foolish, it was wrong, to take so active a part in bringing any two people together. It was adventuring too far, assuming too much, making light of what ought to be serious, a trick of what ought to be simple. She was quite concerned and ashamed, and resolved to do such things no more.

'Here have I,' said she, 'actually talked poor Harriet into being very much attached to this man. She might never have thought of him but for me; and certainly never would have thought of him with hope, if I had not assured her of his attachment, for she is as modest and humble as I used to think him. Oh! that I had been satisfied with persuading her not to accept young Martin. There I was quite right. That was well done of me; but there I should have stopped, and left the rest to time and chance. I was introducing her into good company, and giving her the opportunity of pleasing some one worth having; I ought not to have attempted more. But now, poor girl, her peace is cut up for some time. I have been but half a friend to her.' (*Emma*, chapter 16)

Depending on your age, you will be more or less familiar with the concept of 'shipping'. For those of you for whom this is a novel concept, it is a term used to describe 'fan fictions' that take existing fictional characters and bring them together as a pair. It usually refers to romantic relationships. 'Ship' is short-hand for 'relationSHIP'. Thus, there are fans of *Harry Potter* or *Twilight*, say, who like to write new stories about the series ('fan fic') in which they 'ship' characters like Harry Potter and Hermione together romantically. Fans have enormous fun creating new situations for beloved characters. They can indulge their fantasies about who they think should actually fall in love with whom.

Emma Woodhouse is one kind of 'shipper'. She represents the person who likes to do that in the 'real' world. As a teenager in the eighties, I had a good number of friends who were obsessed with who was 'getting off' with whom and, more to the point, who should be. There was a fair amount of real-life shipping going on. There were even one or two people who liked to act as a kind of broker for love – the well-connected 'cool' kids who could bring two people together and step back and watch what happened. Mostly it was done for good reasons; sometimes for more selfish ones. Either way, it was pretty awful. Being a teenager, in my view, basically sucks and the obsessions at school with dating and first loves was just the worst.

Today's passage shows Emma beginning to question her matchmaking tendencies and skills. This happens in the light of Mr Elton's 'shock' (but very funny) proposal of marriage to her in the back of a carriage, rather than to Harriet. For the reader, there is no shock. The dramatic irony Austen deploys is simply too huge for there to be a doubt: first, despite all Emma's assurances to Harriet that Elton loves her, it is obvious that he is primarily interested in status. Harriet can offer him nothing. Second, at every point we see that Elton is polite to Harriet and attentive to Emma. We see the proposal coming, if not from outer space, then at least from somewhere west of Bath. Emma is shaken, but not yet cured of her matchmaking tendencies. She even toys with trying to 'ship' Harriet with the attorney William Cox. Crucially, she cannot begin to see and read reality clearly, though thankfully she sees that she was wrong in thinking Mr Elton attached to Harriet.

Here she rightly diagnoses what is wrong with her matchmaking: the work of courtship and relationships should flow from the attraction and affection between two people. Mr Elton's courtship of Emma is artificial and ostentatious. His compliments are too good to be true and he shows he is a man after status rather than love. Later in the novel, Frank Churchill's and Emma's flirtatious banter is witty but lacks depth and grip. It indicates no real affinity with its attendant potential for genuine intimacy. Ultimately, it is only Mr Knightley, whose proposal is direct and simple, who shows the model for love to Emma.

How might this passage help us reflect on our pilgrimage through Lent? I want to note the dynamic between Emma's inveterate need to 'ship' her friend and the very slow dawning of her self-understanding of how naughty this is. As a rule, matchmaking is to be avoided. However, the concept of 'shipping' might be helpful in revealing a broader tendency in which we want to centre ourselves in the drama and work of life. Emma may be fictional, but she reveals one version of what Margaret Silf, among others, has called the temptation to live in the 'Kingdom of Self'. This is the realm of self-interest, where we place ourselves and our often-craven desires at the centre. That is all very well when we are playing around with fictional characters as a 'fan fic' writer might; as a writer and fan-fic 'shipper' you get to play – more or less – a kind of minor god. This is part of the joy of being a novelist and fiction writer. However, in your actual relationships with other humans and with yourself, in the long run allowing yourself to give in too consistently to the 'Kingdom of Self' rather than seeking to be a dweller in the Kingdom of God is a way that leads away from the fullness of life. In the Kingdom of God we are in the hands of others, in community; we are, ultimately, in the hands of God. Emma, as she comes to see her world with greater clarity, begins to discover that she is called to find herself in a community of character and grace. As she comes to realize that her life will lie in the hands of Mr Knightley, she begins to step away from the Kingdom of Self. It is a path we too are called to take, whether we are partnered or not. At its richest, it is always a walk towards the Living God.

Living God, you call us into the fullness of life in your Kingdom. When we step away into the Kingdom of Self, call us back to you and our true selves. Amen.

Day 26

'Oh!' cried Emma, 'I know there is not a better creature in the world: but you must allow, that what is good and what is ridiculous are most unfortunately blended in her.'

'They are blended,' said he, 'I acknowledge; and, were she prosperous, I could allow much for the occasional prevalence of the ridiculous over the good. Were she a woman of fortune, I would leave every harmless absurdity to take its chance, I would not quarrel with you for any liberties of manner. Were she your equal in situation—but, Emma, consider how far this is from being the case. She is poor; she has sunk from the comforts she was born to; and, if she live to old age, must probably sink more. Her situation should secure your compassion. It was badly done, indeed! You, whom she had known from an infant, whom she had seen grow up from a period when her notice was an honour, to have you now, in thoughtless spirits, and the pride of the moment, laugh at her, humble her—and before her niece, too—and before others, many of whom (certainly some,) would be entirely guided by your treatment of her.—This is not pleasant to you, Emma— and it is very far from pleasant to me; but I must, I will,—I will tell you truths while I can; satisfied with proving myself your friend by very faithful counsel, and trusting that you will some time or other do me greater justice than you can do now.' (*Emma*, chapter 43)

I know what it is to be mocked and ridiculed. Most of the mockery has centred around my appearance, though some of it has gone deep into the core of my identity. At the risk of using classic English understatement, such ridicule has not been a pleasant experience. Some of the mockery – mostly, these days, deployed anonymously online – has been laughable and childish. I remember being mocked by some Americans for my 'English teeth'. Slightly more difficult to shrug off, especially when I was younger, were comments based on my perceived deviation from Western ideas of beauty and femininity. As someone who transitioned from male to female when I was young, I was often painfully aware of the nastiness of people, usually men, who wanted to humiliate or mock me for not being pretty enough or fitting their idea of what a woman should be. In my head, I always knew it said more about them than me. However, mockery still hurts. These days I care much less. I'm just an average blobby middle-aged woman slowly embracing cronehood. Online, though, the mockery of me as a prominent trans woman can be beyond horrible. It is fair to say that such attacks have, from time to time, damaged my mental health.

I have also mocked others. I attended comedy gigs, especially in my 20s and 30s, when slurs and jokes were used about whole groups of people including, on several occasions, groups I'm part of. I've laughed off the slurs in part to hide myself from being personally targeted. I'm ashamed of my behaviour. As a teenager, I was also a bully and a coward. I was part of a group of people in my sixth form who – and this is no justification – out of our own inadequacy and fear mocked and shamed another person in our school. It was a factor that contributed to that person's breakdown. That was a long time ago and that person and I and others have found a way through to reconciliation and flourishing, but I still feel a mark of appropriate shame.

Why tell you this? Well, the section of *Emma* under consideration today, in which Emma is exposed for her shabby behaviour towards the fussy and vulnerable, yet kind, Miss Bates, speaks very powerfully into my life. Miss Bates lives in genteel poverty with her mother. She witters on with very little focus or purpose. She is – I guess – irritating and tiresome, but she is still a good human being. Emma humiliates her for her prolixity. Are we to judge Emma definitively by her awful and unthinkingly entitled behaviour and cast her out where there is wailing and gnashing of teeth? Or are we to acknowledge that, in the midst of the damage she has caused, there is space for grace and growth? I do hope we are inclined, even in this age where it can feel there is a rapid rush to judgement, to go with the latter. If we're not, I fear we're all in trouble.

Mr Knightley's reprimand to Emma for insulting Miss Bates at the Box Hill picnic is a timely one. Emma realizes the cruelty of her actions and feels appropriate and intense remorse. It is a key moment in Emma's growth in self-understanding. Not only does she recognize how wrongly she has treated Miss Bates, but she begins to recognize her growing attachment to Knightley. It is a huge emotional moment for Emma as she realizes that her reaction to the incident with Miss Bates will bring her closer to or separate her from Knightley. Her reaction takes us directly into her mind, underscoring its seriousness.

We might say that spitefulness or mockery or ridiculing others is part of the natural rough and tumble of life. I guess I've had friendships and relationships where a little verbal wrestling has been fun and part of the friendship. I also enjoy being part of a family that loves to pop my pomposity. However, that is not what we're talking about when we speak of the Miss Bates of this world. This is where entitlement and privilege are used to diminish and ridicule. Jesus might say we are blessed when we are persecuted and reviled for righteousness' sake, but the Kingdom of Heaven invites us into the way of cherishing and delight. There is space in the Body of Christ and the family of God for the likes of Miss Bates, for you and for me. We are called into a community in which we are converted one to another. Difference is never grounds for cruelty. In Christ, we are called to the challenge to dwell in loving grace often precisely with those whom we struggle to respect or like. It is costly, but that way lies the hope of God's New Day.

Patient God, enable me to speak your words of grace and kindness into a troubled world. May the words of my mouth echo the music of your praise. Amen.

Day 27

'[M]ore wonderful things had happened, matches of *greater* disparity had taken place than between Mr. Frank Churchill and me; and, therefore, it seems as if such a thing even as this, may have occurred before—and if I should be so fortunate, beyond expression, as to—if Mr. Knightley should really—if *he* does not mind the disparity, I hope, dear Miss Woodhouse, you will not set yourself against it, and try to put difficulties in the way. But you are too good for that, I am sure.'

Harriet was standing at one of the windows. Emma turned round to look at her in consternation, and hastily said, 'Have you any idea of Mr. Knightley's returning your affection?'

'Yes,' replied Harriet modestly, but not fearfully—'I must say that I have.'

Emma's eyes were instantly withdrawn; and she sat silently meditating, in a fixed attitude, for a few minutes. A few minutes were sufficient for making her acquainted with her own heart. A mind like hers, once opening to suspicion, made rapid progress. She touched—she admitted—she acknowledged the whole truth. Why was it so much worse that Harriet should be in love with Mr. Knightley, than with Frank Churchill? Why was the evil so dreadfully increased by Harriet's having some hope of a return? It darted through her, with the speed of an arrow, that Mr. Knightley must marry no one but herself! (*Emma*, chapter 47)

Emma is undoubtedly bright and her insight has been misdirected towards self-indulgent and over-confident schemes. She consistently misreads reality, assuming that Mr Elton, for example, is attracted to Harriet rather than to herself. Her focus on Harriet's possible matches and her speculations about Jane Fairfax's affections lead her astray. It is only relatively late in the novel – after she realizes that Frank and Jane are engaged – that her perspicacity and insight are properly directed and she makes a quick leap forward in her own self-understanding. Nonetheless, amusingly, she does not come to recognize her love for Knightley on her own; it is her jealousy of Harriet that brings her to self-awareness.

One might call this a 'penny-drop' moment. The conditions finally prevail that enable Emma to read the world and her heart aright. That which has been reasonably clear for us as readers for a while has finally become available to Emma. What enables Emma to find her way to the truth is not a lovely thing: it is jealousy. What this jealousy reminds us of, however, is that there is no short-cut for Emma (or anyone) to maturity and entering into right relationship. The relationship between Emma and Knightley, though based on their private history together, takes shape only in the context of the surrounding web of social relationships. I think this is one of the reasons why the conclusion of the novel is so satisfying: it reminds me that human flourishing is never an abstract matter. The path to wholeness and hope is revealed and pursued in 'real time' through existing and emergent relationships. Jealousy, envy, pride, as much as hope, faith and love, are tokens of embodiment and the cost and joy of being particular bodies existing in time and space. Redemption is no mere concept; it is lived out in specific times and places by humans seeking to make sense of an often bewildering world. We can have 'penny-drop' and 'mic-drop' moments, but they offer focal moments of crisis and opportunity.

The Bible is positively ringing with 'penny-drop' moments. Clarity comes into the midst of disciples like Simon Peter, who offers a touching mix of grip on what God is saying followed by a buffoon's misunderstanding of those purposes. From Moses to Solomon to the Blessed Virgin, from St Elizabeth to Mary Magdalene, the Bible reveals the wonder of insight and reality. Reality is grounded in relationship – with God and with others – and it is the richest motivation to truth-telling and action. I love that moment at the end of John's Gospel (chapter 21) when Peter, the one who had denied Jesus and abandoned his friend and lord, is granted, once again, an opportunity not only to recognize the truth ('It is the Lord') and race ahead of his fellow fishermen, but finally takes up the mantle of responsibility. 'Will you feed my sheep?' Jesus asks, three times. Three times Peter answers affirmatively. Finally, he realizes that his answer must be more than words and he walks out on the path which will lead him to his ultimate sacrifice. Our pilgrimage of grace is not Peter's or the Blessed Virgin's, but it is marked by moments of decision and truth. When the reality of God comes and invites us to step beyond the comfortable places, what will we do? What is the invitation God is making to you, me, us, this day? How might we take better hold on our lives by locating them in his?

Redeeming God, thank you for never giving up on your world. Teach me to act for all that makes for love, and work for your peace and grace. Amen.

Day 28

'My dearest Emma,' said he, 'for dearest you will always be, whatever the event of this hour's conversation, my dearest, most beloved Emma—tell me at once. Say "No," if it is to be said.'—She could really say nothing.—'You are silent,' he cried, with great animation; 'absolutely silent! at present I ask no more.'

Emma was almost ready to sink under the agitation of this moment. The dread of being awakened from the happiest dream, was perhaps the most prominent feeling.

'I cannot make speeches, Emma:' he soon resumed; and in a tone of such sincere, decided, intelligible tenderness as was tolerably convincing.—'If I loved you less, I might be able to talk about it more. But you know what I am.—You hear nothing but truth from me.—I have blamed you, and lectured you, and you have borne it as no other woman in England would have borne it.—Bear with the truths I would tell you now, dearest Emma, as well as you have borne with them. The manner, perhaps, may have as little to recommend them. God knows, I have been a very indifferent lover.—But you understand me.—Yes, you see, you understand my feelings—and will return them if you can. At present, I ask only to hear, once to hear your voice.'

While he spoke, Emma's mind was most busy, and, with all the wonderful velocity of thought, had been able—and yet without losing a word—to catch and comprehend the exact truth of the whole ... Her way was clear, though not quite smooth.—She spoke then, on being so entreated.—What did she say?—Just what she ought, of course. A lady always does.—She said enough to shew there need not be despair—and to invite him to say more himself. He had despaired at one period; he had received such an injunction to caution and silence, as for the time crushed every hope;—she had begun by refusing to hear him.—The change had perhaps been somewhat sudden;—her proposal of taking another turn, her renewing the conversation which she had just put an end to, might be a little extraordinary!—She felt its inconsistency; but Mr. Knightley was so obliging as to put up with it, and seek no farther explanation.

Seldom, very seldom, does complete truth belong to any human disclosure; seldom can it happen that something is not a little disguised, or a little mistaken; but where, as in this case, though the conduct is mistaken, the feelings are not, it may not be very material.—Mr. Knightley could not impute to Emma a more relenting heart than she possessed, or a heart more disposed to accept of his. (*Emma*, chapter 49)

George Knightley's declaration of his love for Emma and Emma's tumbling, brain-fizzing response is surely one of the perfect moments in literature. By the time Knightley speaks, I'm not sure we ever quite thought we'd get there. Equally, there is great pleasure to be found in the exquisite contrast between Knightley's unshowy yet passionate declaration of his love and the way we experience the 'velocity' of Emma's thought processes as she finally grasps reality. This contrast offers us, as readers, relief, joy and amusement, by turn. If some of us have been exasperated by Emma's well-intentioned, if wayward, behaviour or even seen Knightley as a bit of an old fuddy-duddy, all is forgotten and forgiven as we encounter two people whose love is real, equal and tested by life; whose characters and personalities are, ultimately, so beautifully matched and who will enable each other to become more fully their truest selves. Knightley is no orator whose tongue moves on ball bearings, but someone who simply wishes to speak the truth and does so; Emma finds she is called to account by the one person who has never misled or flattered her. Goodness and hope abound. The reality of their love is deeply satisfying.

Seldom, very seldom, does complete truth belong to any human disclosure; seldom can it happen that something is not a little disguised, or a little mistaken; but where, as in this case, though the conduct is mistaken, the feelings are not, it may not be very material.

This is an exquisite piece of Austen wit, refracted through the perspective of the truth-loving Knightley, which offers a smart comment on the messy nature of embodied human truth. When those whose behaviour has somewhat erred, but whose hearts are longing for good, are looked at through the eyes of love and tenderness, a tender rather than a harsh judgement is surely in order. I remember once hearing a journalist claim that the truth has three sides: side one, side two and the third side which lies in the middle. I'm not sure if I entirely buy that analysis, but it certainly captures the slippery and messy nature of what we might call 'embodied truth'. Humans are partial creatures – we see through a mirror dimly, and we are inclined to what is sometimes called 'confirmation bias'. This is the tendency to treat information in a way that confirms or supports our prior beliefs or values. If it is not quite that we see what we want to see, we are the kind of creatures who hold points of view. We can't help ourselves. We are – thankfully – never merely rational, but also affective beings. Not only do we read events through the prism of our own intellectual perspectives and positions, but our hearts impact what we interpret. Austen is right: 'Seldom, very seldom, does complete truth belong to any human disclosure.'

If, at the embodied level, we experience truth as partial and slippery, how much more is that the case as we spend ever greater time in digital space. It is not that I want to suggest that there is some definitive distinction between the embodied and the digital. We are not free-floating intelligences or minds when we are online. Rather, we tend to embody and project ourselves in rather different ways. As someone who has experienced targeted online hate, I am convinced that things which have been said about me would not be said in such a way, if at all, in a face-to-face encounter. There is also significant evidence to suggest that social media algorithms create bunkers in which truth is ever more refracted through the bias. The BBC's Disinformation and Social Media correspondent Marianna Spring has shown, in her work on the BBC's coverage of US Elections as well as in her podcast *Disaster Trolls*, how easy it is for an unsuspecting person to fall down rabbit holes. In these rabbit holes, conspiracy theories like *QAnon* or the claim that the Manchester Arena Bombing was a hoax are pushed as truth. In a world of 'alternative facts', it can be difficult for anyone to resist the truth-twisting of an internet algorithm's smoke and mirrors.

Who and what do we trust? For many of us, to simply answer 'Jesus' will seem too oven-ready. It is an accurate answer, but without analysis and thought the mic-drop answer comes across as the go-to for a five-year-old in the question-time section of the vicar's school assembly. Nonetheless, Jesus says, 'I am the Way, the Truth and the Life.' Part of the gift of understanding Jesus as 'the Truth' is how you immediately find yourself in a place where relationship matters, relationship grounded in trust. To know that Jesus is the Truth requires a recognition that I or we are not the truth. It is an invitation into humility and a letting go of power. There is liberation in this: to be able to admit that we only have a partial grip on the truth, that we see through a mirror dimly and that only *then* shall we see face to face, might be sufficient for us to meet on the ground where Jesus can set us, me, you, free. To be able to centre Jesus – as embodied living truth – might offer the most radical path to reconciliation for those of us bunkered in our beliefs.

Jesus, you are the Way, the Truth and the Life. Thank you for being with me this day and set me free to follow you. Amen.

We feel that we have been blessed far beyond any thing that we have deserved; and though we cannot but pray for a continuance of all these mercies, we acknowledge our unworthiness of them and implore thee to pardon the presumption of our desires. Amen.

JANE AUSTEN

Day 29

Catherine turned away her head, not knowing whether she might venture to laugh. 'I see what you think of me,' said he gravely – 'I shall make but a poor figure in your journal tomorrow.'

'My journal!'

'Yes, I know exactly what you will say: Friday, went to the Lower Rooms; wore my sprigged muslin robe with blue trimmings—plain black shoes—appeared to much advantage; but was strangely harassed by a queer, half-witted man, who would make me dance with him, and distressed me by his nonsense.'

'Indeed I shall say no such thing.'

'Shall I tell you what you ought to say?'

'If you please.'

'I danced with a very agreeable young man, introduced by Mr. King; had a great deal of conversation with him—seems a most extraordinary genius—hope I may know more of him. *That*, madam, is what I *wish* you to say.'

'But, perhaps, I keep no journal.'

'Perhaps you are not sitting in this room, and I am not sitting by you. These are points in which a doubt is equally possible. Not keep a journal! How are your absent cousins to understand the tenour of your life in Bath without one? How are the civilities and compliments of every day to be related as they ought to be, unless noted down every evening in a journal? How are your various dresses to be remembered, and the particular state of your complexion, and curl of your hair to be described in all their diversities, without having constant recourse to a journal?—My dear madam, I am not so ignorant of young ladies' ways as you wish to believe me; it is this delightful habit of journalling which largely contributes

to form the easy style of writing for which ladies are so generally celebrated. Everybody allows that the talent of writing
agreeable letters is peculiarly female. Nature may have done
something, but I am sure it must be essentially assisted by the
practice of keeping a journal.' (*Northanger Abbey*, chapter 3)

The Revd Henry Tilney has a natural teasing wit; it is a dangerous wit that might readily be used to wound. He is the kind of
figure who I suspect might make his bishops a little uncomfortable, not least because they cannot predict quite what he is going
to say next. Humour and wit are always dangerous; they are a
gambit and an invitation to see the world differently. Those
who deploy wit can draw us deeper into the world's possibilities
or make us uncomfortable. Those who are witty are so readily
treated as absurd; indeed, the classical fool has power, but only
by accepting motley. One way the serious and the substantial
have of dealing with their anxieties in the presence of the wit
is to keep them at a distance; one danger for the wit is to turn
their cleverness on the vulnerable. Their witticisms can then
readily resolve into sarcasm and cruelty.

However, in this first encounter between Tilney and Catherine Morland there is as much self-deprecation as mickey-taking.
The socially unsophisticated Catherine is unsure how to react to
his seeming facetiousness. Should she laugh? Should she walk
away? He is a respectable man: she knows that because he is a
clergyman who has been appropriately introduced to her at a
Lower Rooms gathering ... yet he seems oddly mocking of social
conventions. Immediately prior to this exchange, Tilney has
already drawn attention to the artificiality of social discourse,
noting the vacuousness of the usual pleasantries exchanged
between upper-middle-class young men and women. Catherine
wants to laugh at this odd young man. In the excerpt given
here, Tilney goes on to skewer, with more than a little insight,
the gendered conventions of femininity through a witty analysis
of the stereotypical writing habits of genteel young women. His
wit is leavened by a good sprinkling of deprecation, first casting
himself as a social embarrassment and then as a genius. His

self-assessment – toying with masculine stereotypes by simultaneously underplaying and overplaying his hand – enables him to mock the equally shallow cliches of femininity operant in a deeply binaried culture where men and women's behaviour is strictly regulated.

Like many thoughtful young people in every era, Henry Tilney is alert to the absurd, restrictive and arbitrary nature of social convention. Perhaps his use of mockery and sarcasm is a strategy for survival in the face of constricting social obligations that no one of his class can readily escape. Tilney gains a kind of tactical mastery over them by turning them into a joke. His account of a fashionable young woman's enumeration of her dresses and her complexion is funny; he captures a stereotype. He also delineates social restrictions that limit both men and women. Perhaps, in the midst of the social obligations placed on him as a single young man of good family, as well as a clergyman, he hopes to insulate himself from being over-exposed to what he sees as the flimsiness and caprice of fashionable young ladies. What he ultimately finds is that the basic straightforwardness, simplicity and sincerity of Catherine disarms him. Ultimately, they find freedom together in their relationship.

When I was young I often found convention, especially gendered convention, hugely irritating. I grew up in the wake of the Sixties' sexual and cultural revolution. It wasn't as if my world was shaped by the strictures imposed on a Henry Tilney. Class, sexuality, gender were all under negotiation. Nonetheless, as an LGBT+ kid, I found the conservative world of my childhood village beyond restrictive and artificial. The social conventions of expected behaviour for a boy or girl felt weirdly artificial. Convention – understood as 'general agreement on customs, etc., as embodied in accepted standards or usages' (1747) – was increasingly parsed into the negative sense that had emerged by the mid-nineteenth century: convention as artificial behaviour and repression of natural conduct. I just wanted to rebel against rules or practices based on general conduct. I loved to mock and flaunt and transgress established conventions. I was 'naughty' in that satisfying sense we find in the *Book of Common Prayer*.

Where do I sit now? Well, this middle-aged woman knows we cannot live without conventions. Sometimes, and ironically, it is only the restrictions we have that grant us freedom to live well. As evidence consider the impact, in places like the UK and the USA, of politicians who seem to 'get off' from breaking political and ethical conventions for atavistic and opportunistic reasons. Such behaviour breaks up lives and patterns of goodness and hope. Such strategies do not extend the reach of goodness for the most vulnerable; they seek to weaponize resentment and mistrust. There can, then, be a moderating power in social agreements about what constitutes good behaviour.

I suppose the question for us, as much as for Tilney and Catherine, is which conventions and social practices are life-giving. The early fifteenth-century meaning of convention speaks of 'a formal agreement, covenant, treaty', and 'a formal meeting or convention' (of rulers, etc.). I'm not sure to what extent any kind of social or public covenant exists in society anymore. Jesus Christ was prepared to question the contingent social conventions of his own day, but his faithfulness to the deep and abiding obligations of God's covenantal love for Israel were fundamental to who he was. I guess part of the challenge to us, as people seeking to be faithful to the ways of Christ, is to interrogate those things that are incidental to human flourishing and are passing away as much as the bewildering social conventions of Austen's day, as well as those things that lead us ever deeper into the fullness of life. This work of discernment is not simply a Lenten one, but the calling of a lifetime.

Eternal God, help us to focus on the things which abide and which are true. Keep me as the apple of your eye and a seeker after all that leads to life. Amen.

Day 30

'And what are you reading, Miss ——?' 'Oh! it is only a novel!' replies the young lady; while she lays down her book with affected indifference, or momentary shame. — 'It is only Cecilia, or Camilla, or Belinda;' or, in short, only some work in which the greatest powers of the mind are displayed, in which the most thorough knowledge of human nature, the happiest delineation of its varieties, the liveliest effusions of wit and humour, are conveyed to the world in the best-chosen language. Now, had the same young lady been engaged with a volume of the Spectator, instead of such a work, how proudly would she have produced the book, and told its name; though the chances must be against her being occupied by any part of that voluminous publication, of which either the matter or manner would not disgust a young person of taste: the substance of its papers so often consisting in the statement of improbable circumstances, unnatural characters, and topics of conversation which no longer concern anyone living; and their language, too, frequently so coarse as to give no very favourable idea of the age that could endure it. (*Northanger Abbey*, chapter 5)

Part of the fun of *Northanger Abbey* lies in its swipes at the gothic romance novels which it affectionately satirizes. Though they are long forgotten now, the likes of Anne Radcliffe's *The Mysteries of Udolpho* or Fanny Burney's *Camilla* were immensely popular in their day, especially with genteel young women. The basic formula was simple: a beautiful, talented heroine stumbles on a mystery, which builds and builds, along with the characters' and the readers' dread and anxiety, until a startling secret is uncovered, and the young lady lives happily ever after. Think *Twilight* with fewer vampires and a cooler heroine. In casting the slightly hapless (and not very talented) Catherine as the heroine in a novel that both satirizes and performs a gothic romance, Austen mocks the gothic and offers a wonderful tribute to the power of the over-charged plot and the happy ending.

In Austen's time, novels were typically looked down upon, especially by those of the upper class. A journal like *The Spectator* was considered much better reading fodder. It was only later in the nineteenth century that the novel triumphed. Indeed, in the late eighteenth and early nineteenth century, it was the poet who was supreme. Poets could earn superstar royalties. Part of what Austen does with *Northanger Abbey* is to take a still slightly disreputable form and relocate it in a pleasing new light. She shows what even the sensational novel can look like in the hands of a genius. She begins both to redeem fiction and play her part in establishing the novel on a new level. She creates characters which last and have sufficient suppleness to remain memorable.

Not least of the concerns about the showy trash fiction of Austen's day was that it was hardly edifying. I guess that in the context of a good and holy Lent, edification is a high priority. It is a reason why one chooses a Lent book like this to study rather than a dubious airport novel. Edification has implications of building up and construction and creating a structure. The religious sense has implications of building up the soul, although by Austen's time the concept of edification would cover mental improvement too. Reading highly emotional, sensationalist novels is hardly edifying. However, I think we should be cautious about being too pious and snobby about other people's reading habits. One of the things to be alert to is the gendered nature of much snobbiness. From *Camilla* to *Mallory Towers* to *Twilight* – whatever their literary merits or lack of them – girls' reading habits have suffered in comparison to those books pushed at boys. Part of the pleasure of *Northanger Abbey* is that the sophisticated Henry Tilney loves a good gothic romance himself.

DAY 30

I suppose fiction itself might be read as lacking in moral purpose or seriousness or insight. We might make it problematic
just as the Puritan mind-set made theatre problematic. Austen,
of course, launches a pre-emptive attack on such an attitude,
waspishly stating that a novel may be 'work in which the
greatest powers of the mind are displayed, in which the most
thorough knowledge of human nature, the happiest delineation
of its varieties, the liveliest effusions of wit and humour, are
conveyed to the world in the best-chosen language'. I adore
the Bible and remain in awe of Jesus' creativity and genius
for inviting his audience into imaginative space, but I remain
convinced that we have nothing to fear from other kinds
of literature. A theme of this book has been how, when we
draw closer to Christ, we draw closer to reality. We become
more truly ourselves. I do not think that should be a grim and
grinding work. Escapism and imagination are part of God's
endowment to our species. As C. S. Lewis says, 'Literature adds
to reality, it does not simply describe it. It enriches the necessary competencies that daily life requires and provides; and in
this respect, it irrigates the deserts that our lives have already
become.' Perhaps I should give the final word to Jane herself:
'The person, be it gentleman or lady, who has not pleasure in a
good novel, must be intolerably stupid.'

*God of Life, you long to irrigate the deserts of our lives. By your
grace, may I receive your Living Water with gladness. Amen.*

Day 31

The advantages of natural folly in a beautiful girl have been already set forth by the capital pen of a sister author;—and to her treatment of the subject I will only add, in justice to men, that though to the larger and more trifling part of the sex, imbecility in females is a great enhancement of their personal charms, there is a portion of them too reasonable and too well informed themselves to desire anything more in woman than ignorance. But Catherine did not know her own advantages—did not know that a good-looking girl, with an affectionate heart and a very ignorant mind, cannot fail of attracting a clever young man, unless circumstances are particularly untoward. In the present instance, she confessed and lamented her want of knowledge, declared that she would give anything in the world to be able to draw; and a lecture on the picturesque immediately followed, in which his instructions were so clear that she soon began to see beauty in everything admired by him, and her attention was so earnest that he became perfectly satisfied of her having a great deal of natural taste. (*Northanger Abbey*, chapter 14)

Recently I read that *Northanger Abbey* had received a 'content warning' from Greenwich University for containing 'sexism' and 'gender stereotypes'. I guess that this is one of those passages which, if the report was true, generated that warning. Of course, truth is that Austen was mocking those gender roles rather than upholding them. This passage – which takes place during Catherine and the Tilneys' walk around Beechen Cliff – deliciously unpicks the representation of femininity in Fanny Burney's *Camilla*. Catherine, who has been cast as the heroine, is – with tender and loving satire – not talented enough to play the heroine à *la* Burney's Indiana. Catherine undermines the stereotype by not being able to play the stereotype. She is – across the arc of the novel – permitted a three-dimensional character and fate.

Austen, then, in this passage quietly and savagely critiques the 'bimbofication' of women in a patriarchal society. That is, she exposes the extent to which, in her society (no less than ours), the social and cultural value of women was read through the scope of male priorities; a woman was subject to the male gaze and, if she wanted to get on within the narrow opportunities afforded her, she had better seek to fit the expectations of a male-orientated society. The naive and poorly educated Catherine is, in this scene, ill-equipped to read nature in the terms then fashionable: the picturesque. This provides Tilney the opportunity to fill that gap with his mastery: he instructs her emptiness in such a way that she begins to see the world through his eyes and perspective. However, when we read this passage with the irony we know Austen brought to bear in all her writings, we see critique rather than approval. This passage does not praise vapidity but exposes the price women pay under conditions where vapidity is expected as a survival technique.

It would be absurd to imagine that we can – simply by an act of will – escape the social and religious conventions and tropes within which we live. Any number of texts in the Bible have been read as legitimating the oppression and subjugation of women. Those texts have themselves become part of the substrate of society. Often the Bible and Christian tradition have been used to legitimate social attitudes that treat women as lesser and secondary. I suppose that one thing the University of Greenwich story reminds us of is that social conventions have shifted so significantly over time that – without the subtlety that an ironic reading brings to a text – those things that are only seemingly true in Austen's text are read as toxic. Rightly so, I think. Not least of the disturbing aspects of our so-called progressive society is how unprogressive so many attitudes towards women remain. There are still very many people, often young men, who feel comfortable with patriarchal understandings of relationships and who are threatened by any sign of progress; women continue to be treated as playthings by men, and women still feel they can make better headway in a prejudiced society by playing up to feminine stereotypes.

I want to suggest that to follow Jesus requires a critique and exposure of the pernicious effects of stereotypes of femininity and masculinity every bit as biting as Austen's. I believe the Bible offers one route for liberative theology. It is no mere text of terror. It holds the seeds of our liberation from toxic patriarchal conceptions of identity which ruin and limit us. Jesus, however, models a way of being fully human that subverts a key problem that has damaging effects not just for women and girls, but for boys and men: toxic masculinity. Consider Jesus' death on a cross. It would have been coded in Roman Imperial culture as shameful. Why? Because it reduced a man to a passive, humiliating death coded as suitable only for a woman. While it is clearly wrong to suggest that being a woman should be parsed as 'passivity', the fact that Christ embraces the position assigned to women in his day is quite a moment: the abiding gender stereotype which says that men are shamed by passivity is turned upside down.

Equally, Jesus shows on the cross abiding solidarity with women, those to whom violence and exploitation are most likely to happen. It should come as no surprise that his death is witnessed primarily by women disciples. At the cross, Christ and the women stand in solidarity with one another. There is mutual recognition. The women will not abandon one whom they recognize as placed in a position they know only too well. When Jesus says, from the cross, 'My God, why have you forsaken me?' I think he cries out to the God who needs to die: the patriarchal God who only values power and power-over; who is the God of macho force and action. In that moment, I wonder if Jesus and the women of the cross discover the Living God: the God of relationship and solidarity. This is the God found among those who stand by one another in their hour of need and will not give up until hope is found. Is it any surprise, then, that the first witnesses to Christ's resurrection were women?

Holy God, help me to walk the way of the cross of Jesus this day. As I let go of my way, may I find the path to life in your holy Way. Amen.

Day 32

Isabella now entered the room with so eager a step, and a look of such happy importance, as engaged all her friend's notice. Maria was without ceremony sent away, and Isabella, embracing Catherine, thus began:— 'Yes, my dear Catherine, it is so indeed; your penetration has not deceived you.—Oh! that arch eye of yours!—It sees through every thing.'

Catherine replied only by a look of wondering ignorance.

'Nay, my beloved, sweetest friend,' continued the other, 'compose yourself.—I am amazingly agitated, as you perceive. Let us sit down and talk in comfort. Well, and so you guessed it the moment you had my note?—Sly creature!—Oh! my dear Catherine, you alone, who know my heart, can judge of my present happiness. Your brother is the most charming of men. I only wish I were more worthy of him.—But what will your excellent father and mother say?—Oh! heavens! when I think of them I am so agitated!' (*Northanger Abbey*, chapter 15)

Isabella Thorpe, the speaker, has been flirting with Catherine's brother, James, for nearly a week. They have become engaged, and Isabella is just about to tell Catherine. Isabella assumes that Catherine is as gossipy and sharp as she is herself. Of course we, as readers, have come to realize that Catherine is not terribly perceptive and here she has no idea what Isabella is talking about. The passage amusingly demonstrates Catherine's flawed powers of perception. She cannot fathom the motivations of people, particularly when they are negative, and she cannot read people or their behaviour. In this case, she did not guess at the engagement that the entire town of Bath assumed was imminent. Her obliviousness stems from a combination of naïveté and innocence. Catherine needs more experience and a better understanding of what drives people before she can make accurate assumptions about how they will behave.

Many of us will have been guilty of Isabella's love for gossip. Some of us may perhaps have been as naive and innocent as Catherine. There is no sin in being a little naive and slow on the uptake. Innocence has its place. It has implications of purity, blamelessness and simplicity. It is risky, of course, without a leavening of wisdom. As for gossip? Is there really anything so bad about Isabella's love of whispers and scandal? I suspect most of us will want to cut her a little slack. She's a young woman and many of us, when we were teenagers, indulged in a light-hearted, chatty bit of gossip about who was going out with whom or what the 'latest goss' about 'x, y or z' was ... It would be priggish, wouldn't it, to seek to police the youthful excitement of those who wish to speculate on the ins and outs of relationships? I am certainly tempted to think so.

St Paul, in 2 Corinthians, is less sanguine about gossip. He writes anxiously about what he will find when he visits the church in Corinth for a third time. He fears that there will be quarrelling and jealousy, slander and gossip and disorder. The word he uses for gossip is the Greek *koine* for a 'whispering'. It is sometimes used to refer to the murmurings of a snake charmer. He is worried that, should he visit, he will not be seen as he ought – as an apostle of Jesus who comes to build them up. He is equally worried that he will find a community in decay, unable to live up to the vocation in Christ to which they have been called and in which they have been formed. Paul fears that the unity found in Christ will have been fractured by human self-interest and sin. Malicious whispers will have damaged fellowship.

It is more than a little easy to parse the account of gossip covered by Paul in 2 Corinthians into a false equivalence with Isabella's 'gossip girl' persona. I have no desire to do that. A bit of 'goss' about who is going out with whom is surely on a totally different level to the malicious whispering that can salt the good and holy ground of God's community. However, I do know from experience how rapidly gossip can spill out of control and be used to diminish and traduce people and inflame situations. That is the thing about whispers, fun and silly though they can seem. The seemingly silly gossip we indulge in at any age can so rapidly become the means for destroying the reputations of those who lack power. Social media and the internet only amplify that grim possibility. I suppose that this ugly possibility – where what looks like fun gossip metastasizes into ugly whispers – invites us all to a considered caution. Our tongues and the tongues of others can wound. Our whispers about others and theirs about us can seem harmless and fun. Sometimes they may even be as innocent as Catherine Morland's at this point in *Northanger Abbey*. I suspect a more considered appreciation of whether our remarks seek to love our neighbour as ourselves might indicate otherwise.

God of Truth, lead me ever deeper on to your holy ground. As I step further along your Way, help me grow more into the likeness of Jesus Christ. Amen.

Day 33

After an evening, the little variety and seeming length of which made her peculiarly sensible of Henry's importance among them, she was heartily glad to be dismissed; though it was a look from the General not designed for her observation which sent his daughter to the bell. When the butler would have lit his master's candle, however, he was forbidden. The latter was not going to retire. 'I have many pamphlets to finish,' said he to Catherine, 'before I can close my eyes, and perhaps may be poring over the affairs of the nation for hours after you are asleep. Can either of us be more meetly employed? My eyes will be blinding for the good of others, and *yours* preparing by rest for future mischief.'

But neither the business alleged, nor the magnificent compliment, could win Catherine from thinking that some very different object must occasion so serious a delay of proper repose. To be kept up for hours, after the family were in bed, by stupid pamphlets was not very likely. There must be some deeper cause: something was to be done which could be done only while the household slept; and the probability that Mrs. Tilney yet lived, shut up for causes unknown, and receiving from the pitiless hands of her husband a nightly supply of coarse food, was the conclusion which necessarily followed. Shocking as was the idea, it was at least better than a death unfairly hastened, as, in the natural course of things, she must ere long be released. The suddenness of her reputed illness, the absence of her daughter, and probably of her other children, at the time—all favoured the supposition of her imprisonment. Its origin—jealousy perhaps, or wanton cruelty—was yet to be unravelled. (*Northanger Abbey*, chapter 23)

Northanger Abbey is a witty study in, and satire of, the febrile imagination. Austen takes the classic tropes of the gothic romance – crucially the deep, dark secret exposed by the hero-ine – and lovingly reveals them for the overheated plot devices they are. As the passage above reveals, Catherine has so deeply accepted the gothic idea of the 'secret plot' that she cannot accept that General Tilney is not caught up in some dreadful shenanigans. Catherine is convinced that he must either have murdered his wife or – shock! – has her secretly locked up against her will. She purposes to find out more, scaring herself silly in the process (and not without pleasure I hasten to add!). She discovers, in the shadowy old house, precisely no sign of naughtiness ... indeed, there is a comedy moment when she discovers in an old box a piece of 'parchment' that begins with the dread word ... 'socks'. Catherine has found a laundry list! This silliness is both symbolic of her lovableness and a key step on her journey to growing up.[1]

There is nothing wrong with enjoying the satire and silliness in Austen's treatment of the gothic novel. We might, however, raise an eyebrow at this aspect of *Northanger Abbey* featuring as a focus for reflection in a Lent book. Well, I think that Austen, in putting a spotlight on suggestibility and febrile imagination, invites a deeper dive into modern concerns than we might at first believe. I recognize that Catherine's ridiculously over-the-top reactions to the books she loves is unlikely to affect many of those who read and study this book. However, I think we're fools if we imagine that a great many people, quite possibly including us from time to time, are above suggestibility and over-excitement. Tempting though it might be to picture our-selves as entirely rational, surely the history of human behaviour

---

1 In defence of Catherine's love of reading it is worth saying this: if her febrile ideas about the wickedness of the General are generated by her reading of gothic novels, isn't her judgement ultimately proven (basically) correct? He does behave infamously by throwing her out of the Abbey when he realizes she is not an heiress. After Catherine's belief that Mrs Tilney has been murdered or locked up has been proven false, Henry counsels, 'Consult your own understanding, your own sense of the probable.' Catherine's judgement is better refined than he thinks. Indeed, she realizes that ultimately 'she has scarcely sinned against [the General's] character, or magnified his cruelty'.

shows that we are as much affective as rational creatures. Algorithms and apps depend on our impulsive love of clicking links. If most of us are able to resist the seductions of conspiracy theories, I'm not sure we are as immune to fake news and post-truth as some of us think we are. I have seen moral panics about trans people and LGBT+ people take root online in ways I never thought possible a few years ago. Even if that is predicated on fake accounts and bots pushing nonsense on sites like Twitter (X), it nonetheless reveals how readily ordinary, intelligent human beings are suggestible to propaganda techniques.

The Catholic wing of the Church, drawing on the wisdom of St Thomas Aquinas, tends to talk about the importance of cultivating character and the virtues. Human flourishing is a matter of formation. Evangelicals speak more about cultivating holiness. Both wings of the Church share a moral, personal and social seriousness. They are determined to remind us of our vocation to be those who centre their lives on Christ. As we are formed into his likeness we are not called to be like robots or machines. Nor are we called to be gullible. The vocation is – as St Paul reminds us – to undertake an appropriate testing of reality. In Galatians 6, he reminds us to bear one another's burdens. When we do this, we will fulfil the law of Christ. This requires testing: an interrogation of one's own contribution to the life of the community. Good judgement and wisdom cannot be dispensed with. Some of us, of course, will be more credulous than others; some will be more cynical. The real purpose of good judgement, though – as that which might, just might, protect us from suggestibility and foolishness – is to lead us closer to Christ. Jesus reminds us to be innocent as doves and wise as serpents. We are not called to be gullible; rather our vocation is to head towards Christ who is the truth. What can we do today to ensure we stay close to that truth?

O Holy Wisdom of God, you long for us to centre our lives on Jesus Christ. In mercy and grace, help me rejoice as I share in the burdens of love to which the Church is called today. Amen.

Day 34

Sir Walter Elliot, of Kellynch Hall, in Somersetshire, was a man who, for his own amusement, never took up any book but the Baronetage; there he found occupation for an idle hour, and consolation in a distressed one; there his faculties were roused into admiration and respect, by contemplating the limited remnant of the earliest patents; there any unwelcome sensations, arising from domestic affairs, changed naturally into pity and contempt as he turned over the almost endless creations of the last century; and there, if every other leaf were powerless, he could read his own history with an interest which never failed. This was the page at which the favourite volume always opened:

'ELLIOT OF KELLYNCH HALL.

'Walter Elliot, born March 1, 1760, married, July 15, 1784, Elizabeth, daughter of James Stevenson, Esq. of South Park, in the county of Gloucester, by which lady (who died 1800) he has issue Elizabeth, born June 1, 1785; Anne, born August 9, 1787; a still-born son, November 5, 1789; Mary, born November 20, 1791.' ...

Vanity was the beginning and the end of Sir Walter Elliot's character; vanity of person and of situation. He had been remarkably handsome in his youth; and, at fifty-four, was still a very fine man. Few women could think more of their personal appearance than he did, nor could the valet of any new made lord be more delighted with the place he held in society. He considered the blessing of beauty as inferior only to the blessing of a baronetcy; and the Sir Walter Elliot, who united these gifts, was the constant object of his warmest respect and devotion. (*Persuasion*, chapter 1)

The opening paragraphs of *Persuasion* are a satire on Anne Elliot's father, Sir Walter. Austen sets up the novel with a satisfying takedown of vain aristocrats and the upper classes. This attack is so broad, a casual reader might assume that the novel is of eighteenth-century provenance rather than signalling the emergence of the confident realistic nineteenth-century novel. Sir Walter is a dreadful man – vanity was the beginning and the end of his character – and along with his awful eldest daughter Elizabeth and the self-pitying younger daughter Mary, he is set up as a potent contrast to the novel's central character, Anne. From the outset, we can be in no doubt about both the satiric potential of Sir Walter and the serious implications of the self-centredness of this vainglorious popinjay.

Is Sir Walter too dreadful to be believed? His self-obsession runs through both his shallow fascination with his own good looks and the attention he gives to his heritage as a member of one of the oldest families in the Baronetage. Austen's barbs fall especially well, given that she locates Elliot as a member of the lowest rank of those who inherit titles. He is acutely aware of gradations of rank and he clings on to the fact that his name is older than many of higher rank. His sense of position and vanity contribute to Anne's disastrous decision to break off her engagement to Wentworth, a man whom we shall soon discover is justifiably still angry with Anne eight years on. Under the influence of Lady Russell, family friend and de facto mother-figure for Anne, Sir Walter had been persuaded that Wentworth was not good enough for Anne. Wentworth, after all, was a low-ranking officer in the Navy, without name, fortune or rank. Sir Walter's prejudices against the Navy are revealed later in the book when – due to his profligacy with money – he has to rent out his ancestral home to, of all people, an admiral and his wife (who happens to be the sister of Wentworth). Not least among Sir Walter's objections to the Navy is the fact that being a sailor ruins one's complexion! No amount of powder will fix the tan a sailor supposedly acquires at sea.

If Sir Walter is a broad-brushed fool, what leaps out at me is how he almost seems made for the times we live in now.

If we don't spend time looking at the Book of Baronetage or Burke's Peerage for reassurance or comfort about our place in the world, most of us orientate our lives around our own social media feeds. We lose hours, sometimes days, checking out what those whom we think important are saying or – if we think we're quite important – what others are saying in response to our posts. We talk about 'my feed' or 'my timeline'. We live, also, in a time when many of us feel encouraged to curate our identities online and live our 'best lives', all filtered through air-brushed photos of ourselves on Instagram. Just as a Walter Elliot might commission a portrait of himself showing his best side, so do many of us love a good selfie. Vanity has been democratized.

Vanity is a kind of emptiness and conceitedness. The Preacher in Ecclesiastes famously says, 'Vanity of vanities … all is vanity.' This does not quite have the implications of conceitedness we might associate with Sir Walter. It has implications of futility and emptiness, in which all endeavour ultimately resolves into nothing. Our attempts to weld the world into the shape of our desires is ultimately in vain. The emptiness of vanity should challenge all of us. Vanity is likely to be with us until the end of time. It is a bone-deep, species-level problem. Where there are opportunities for politicians, influencers, narcissists and, well, the rest of us to indulge in fanning our self-image, evidence suggests that we shall take them. However, to remember the essential void-like nature of vanity is an immensely helpful corrective. 'Like a dog returns to its vomit, so a fool returns to his folly' (Prov. 26.11). The same applies to vanity. The distorting mirror of our emptiness will only make us long for more; the food to be found at vanity's table does not satisfy. There is, of course, another table; there is another likeness into which we are called to grow.

Creator God, thank you that we are made in your image of love. Through Jesus Christ, help us turn away from sin and follow you, dependent on your mercy and grace. Amen.

For all whom we love and value, for every friend and connection, we equally pray; however divided and far asunder, we know that we are alike before thee, and under thine eye. May we be equally united in thy faith and fear, in fervent devotion towards thee, and in thy merciful protection this night. Pardon oh Lord! the imperfections of these our prayers, and accept them through the mediation of our blessed saviour. Amen.

JANE AUSTEN

Day 35

Mrs. Croft, though neither tall nor fat, had a squareness, up-rightness, and vigour of form, which gave importance to her person. She had bright dark eyes, good teeth, and altogether an agreeable face; though her reddened and weather-beaten complexion, the consequence of her having been almost as much at sea as her husband, made her seem to have lived some years longer in the world than her real eight-and-thirty. Her manners were open, easy, and decided, like one who had no distrust of herself, and no doubts of what to do; without any approach to coarseness, however, or any want of good humour. Anne gave her credit, indeed, for feelings of great consideration towards herself, in all that related to Kellynch, and it pleased her: especially, as she had satisfied herself in the very first half minute, in the instant even of introduction, that there was not the smallest symptom of any knowledge or suspicion on Mrs. Croft's side, to give a bias of any sort. She was quite easy on that head, and consequently full of strength and courage, till for a moment electrified by Mrs. Croft's suddenly saying, 'It was you, and not your sister, I find, that my brother had the pleasure of being acquainted with, when he was in this country.'

Anne hoped she had outlived the age of blushing; but the age of emotion she certainly had not.

'Perhaps you may not have heard that he is married?' added Mrs. Croft. (*Persuasion*, chapter 6)

Jane Austen's writing is sometimes accused of lacking proper drama and plot. Certainly, she is not an adrenaline-fuelled thriller writer, or an author of incident-packed chick-lit. Indeed, *Northanger Abbey* is a kind of mickey-take of the action-packed gothic novels fashionable in her youth. Nonetheless, I get why some people think that nothing much happens in Austen's novels. Perhaps that's why some recent 'adaptations' such as the execrable Netflix version of *Persuasion* or the downright silly *Pride and Prejudice and Zombies* seek to up the stakes.

For those of us, however, who've bought deeply into Austen's oeuvre, the vignette above offers a genuine heart-in-mouth moment. After her father and her sister Elizabeth have quit the ancestral home of Kellynch Hall, with a view to it being tenanted by Admiral Croft and his wife, Anne Elliot goes to stay with her other sister Mary Musgrove and her family. When Admiral and Mrs Croft have taken up residence, Anne makes a social call back to Kellynch. This vignette captures Anne's first encounter with the plain-speaking and essentially likeable Mrs Croft. Anne has done her best to come to terms with the fallout from the one big decision of her life: to break off her engagement, eight years previously, to Frederick Wentworth. The encounter with Mrs Croft brings Anne back into the orbit of the man from whom she broke away and whom she has sought to forget. For Frederick Wentworth is a brother of Mrs Croft's. Thus, as this scene unfolds, we find ourselves caught up in Anne's heart-stopping moment: the news that the man she still secretly desires has got married. Of course, almost immediately we discover that the report is mistaken. Frederick has not got married. The newlywed is Mrs Croft's other brother. I don't think that she is toying with Anne, wanting to get a rise or reaction out of her. She has made, in her straightforward, direct way, an honest mistake. Nonetheless, it is a telling moment.

Part of the joy as well as the challenge of *Persuasion* is captured in this exquisite line, 'Anne hoped she had outlived the age of blushing; but the age of emotion she certainly had not.' *Persuasion* is absolutely not some hot-blooded romance, a Mills and Boon for the Georgian set. It is a study in mature and life-worn desire. This is part of its genius, indeed its originality as a feminist text. It dares to centre a woman who is a grown-up, past (in patriarchal terms) her first desirability, and yet whose longings and love are the emotional lodestone of the story. It is, also, part of the challenge *Persuasion* presents to those of us who are mesmerized by the freshness and witty simplicity of Austen's early novels, especially *Pride and Prejudice*. Anne has outlived the age of blushing, but not the age of emotion. There is no sin in blushing or in being a young woman who (stereotypically) does this, but in a world where women are stereotyped, I rejoice in a woman who is permitted mature emotions.

Christian faith, in one sense, is not about being a grown-up or being mature. Jesus speaks of becoming like a little child; we are encouraged into an intimate address to God as father, indeed as 'Abba' or 'Dadda'. If being mature or grown-up is about being cynical or having a heart that is sealed-up from the world, then surely being a Christian requires resistance to such adulthood. It is not that we are called to become simperers or fools, but rather that, in Christ, we remain open to others and especially to the ultimate Other, God. I should not wish to escape the 'age of emotion' and nor should you.

The mature heart, aware of the unavoidability of the 'age of emotion', is one that has been tested and knows the vicissitudes of this costly, heart-shredding world and, nonetheless, persists. It is a vocational heart that requires renewal, not least in the company of friends and those who cherish us; it requires finding rest in prayer and God's cherishing. That path, the path of the heart committed to the vocation of love and openness to others, is one we can so readily be deflected from. In the face of life's trials, the vocational heart can sometimes barely see the way ahead. The person who seeks the way of God often has no more insight into the way ahead than Anne Elliot at the start of *Persuasion*. But nonetheless she persists, hurt and worried though she is. Those of us who are beyond the beginnings – the age of blushing – and want to be honest about what is required to be faithful to the God of Love could do worse than reflect on this line attributed to Hildegard of Bingen: 'Love abounds in all things, excels from the depths to beyond the stars, is lovingly disposed to all things. She has given the king on high the kiss of peace.'

God of Surpassing Peace, teach me to rest in you. Educate my heart that I may receive a little more of your grace this day, and rejoice in your love which abounds in all things. Amen.

Day 36

'Your sister is an amiable creature; but yours is the character of decision and firmness, I see. If you value her conduct or happiness, infuse as much of your own spirit into her as you can. But this, no doubt, you have been always doing. It is the worst evil of too yielding and indecisive a character, that no influence over it can be depended on. You are never sure of a good impression being durable; everybody may sway it. Let those who would be happy be firm. Here is a nut,' said he, catching one down from an upper bough, 'to exemplify: a beautiful glossy nut, which, blessed with original strength, has outlived all the storms of autumn. Not a puncture, not a weak spot anywhere. This nut,' he continued, with playful solemnity, 'while so many of his brethren have fallen and been trodden under foot, is still in possession of all the happiness that a hazel nut can be supposed capable of.' Then returning to his former earnest tone—'My first wish for all whom I am interested in, is that they should be firm. If Louisa Musgrove would be beautiful and happy in her November of life, she will cherish all her present powers of mind.'

He had done, and was unanswered. (*Persuasion*, chapter 10)

During a long walk out to Winthrop, Anne tires and sits down. As she rests, she overhears a conversation between Captain Wentworth and Louisa. It is during this conversation that Louisa reveals – to the shock of Wentworth – that Anne turned down Charles Musgrove, the future husband of Anne's sister, Mary. It is in this exchange that Anne realizes that Wentworth is still angry with her.

However, prior to Louisa's revelation, Wentworth and Louisa discuss character. Louisa considers her sister Henrietta lacking in

determination and boldness. Wentworth, flirtatiously attracted
to the lively Louisa, commends her fearlessness and firmness.
He says, 'let those who would be happy be firm' and uses the
example of a hazelnut to playfully demonstrate his point. What
is especially satisfying about this exchange is the way that –
unknowingly – Wentworth describes Anne's mature character.
His understanding of her, at this point of the novel, is framed
– not unreasonably – in terms of her rejection of him eight years
before. Perhaps, in his mind, the analogy of the hazelnut is also
a work of contrast between who he (unrealistically) imagines
Louisa to be and the person he has experienced Anne not to be.
However, in those eight years of separation, Anne has proven
firm and fearless. She has turned down the good and respectable offer of marriage from Charles Musgrove; in her sadness
and depression she has found a determination and steel Wentworth cannot yet grasp. The analogy of the hazelnut prefigures
the truth of Anne's character.

Thomas Merton suggests that, ultimately, we are called to be
our true selves. There is a problem, however: for us as humans
to be our true selves is a tricky business. Merton suggests that
each of us can give no greater glory to God than being ourselves – our true selves.[1] He offers the example of a tree to
clarify the simplicity and challenge of being our true selves. A
tree, he suggests, gives glory to God by being a tree. However,
for the tree that is not a difficult thing. It cannot be other than
its essential 'tree-ness'. For humans, however, it can be terribly
complicated. We have choices, multiple paths and possibilities
before us; we are marked with sin. So the only way any of us
can know and be truly ourselves is to know ourselves in God.
For only God sees the picture clearly. A journey into self is a
journey into God.

We struggle, then, to be like Wentworth's hazelnut. The
human vocation to follow Jesus Christ requires us to recognize
how readily we step from the path of the Living God and, in

---

1 Thomas Merton, *Seeds of Contemplation* (London: Burns & Oates,
1962), chapter 2.

trust and grace, seek after the way of God again. We are rarely as steadfast as we might be. Anne's faithfulness and firmness is remarkable. She has been tested in the fire of loss and sadness. In her love, she has remained consistent and faithful, but has also – Wentworth is yet to realize – become much more. She has found in the losses and depredations of the world a heart still capable of love. That's a vocation indeed. She has not become shrivelled up and bitter. If her situation has become desperate – and there is no doubt that she has become deeply submerged in her seeming loss of Wentworth – she still holds out the hope of the Living Water of love that shall lead to blooms in the desert.

Centuries before Austen, Mother Julian of Norwich offered her own profound meditation on a hazelnut. In her First Revelation, Jesus helps her picture the whole of creation as like a hazelnut. I leave you with Julian's meditation, inviting you to consider how what she says speaks as much truth about our own little lives as of the whole of creation:

> In this Revelation he showed me something else, a tiny thing, no bigger than a hazelnut, lying in the palm of my hand, and as round as any ball. I looked at it, puzzled, and thought: 'What is it?' The answer came: 'It is everything that is made.' I wondered how it could survive. It was so small that I expected it to shrivel up and disappear. Then I was answered: 'It exists now and always because God loves it.' Thus I understood that everything exists through the love of God.[2]

Faithful God, in you all things shall be well and all manner of things. May I have the trust to hold to that truth and promise this day. Amen.

---

2 Mother Julian of Norwich, *Revelations of Divine Love*, ed. Halcyon Backhouse and Rhonda Pipe (London: Hodder, 1987), p. 13.

Day 37

'Is there no one to help me?' were the first words which burst from Captain Wentworth, in a tone of despair, and as if all his own strength were gone.

'Go to him, go to him,' cried Anne, 'for heaven's sake go to him. I can support her myself. Leave me, and go to him. Rub her hands, rub her temples; here are salts; take them, take them.'

Captain Benwick obeyed, and Charles at the same moment, disengaging himself from his wife, they were both with him; and Louisa was raised up and supported more firmly between them, and everything was done that Anne had prompted, but in vain; while Captain Wentworth, staggering against the wall for his support, exclaimed in the bitterest agony—

'Oh God! her father and mother!'

'A surgeon!' said Anne.

He caught the word; it seemed to rouse him at once, and saying only—'True, true, a surgeon this instant,' was darting away, when Anne eagerly suggested—

'Captain Benwick, would not it be better for Captain Benwick? He knows where a surgeon is to be found.'

Every one capable of thinking felt the advantage of the idea, and in a moment (it was all done in rapid moments) Captain Benwick had resigned the poor corpse-like figure entirely to the brother's care, and was off for the town with the utmost rapidity.

As to the wretched party left behind, it could scarcely be said which of the three, who were completely rational, was suffering most: Captain Wentworth, Anne, or Charles, who, really a very affectionate brother, hung over Louisa with sobs of grief, and could only turn his eyes from one sister, to see the other in a state as insensible, or to witness the hysterical agitations of his wife, calling on him for help which he could not give.

Anne, attending with all the strength and zeal, and thought, which instinct supplied, to Henrietta, still tried, at intervals, to suggest comfort to the others, tried to quiet Mary, to animate Charles, to assuage the feelings of Captain Wentworth. Both seemed to look to her for directions.

'Anne, Anne,' cried Charles, 'What is to be done next? What, in heaven's name, is to be done next?'

Captain Wentworth's eyes were also turned towards her. (*Persuasion*, chapter 12)

There is no doubt that in Austen's day, as much as our own, women negotiated what is often called the Male Gaze. The value of women, and young middle-class women on the marriage 'mart' in particular, was determined in powerfully toxic ways in terms of looks and the manner in which she held herself in the world. Conventional beauty and loveliness were readily translated into goodness and value. Women were valued for elegance, good looks and manners. Her accomplishments – drawing, playing the piano, singing and speaking French – were ornamental.

This scene is important as a pivot point in the story. Wentworth, Anne and the younger Musgroves have gone to Lyme Regis to visit Wentworth's old naval friends, Harville and Benwick. Immediately prior to this exchange, Louisa Musgrove – with whom Wentworth has been flirting – has fallen from the Cobb, the harbour wall. Louisa had insisted on jumping down the steep stairs, assisted by Wentworth. Despite Wentworth's advice against doing so on this occasion, not least due to the windy weather, Louisa insists on doing so. This is typical Louisa: 'In all their walks, he had had to jump her from the stiles; the sensation was delightful to her.' All goes wrong in an instant:

She fell on the pavement on the Lower Cobb, and was taken up lifeless! There was no wound, no blood, no visible bruise; but her eyes were closed, she breathed not, her face was like death. The horror of the moment to all who stood around!

The incident at the Cobb is telling. Louisa Musgrove is a young woman of 19. Her liveliness has an allure, certainly for Wentworth. She is – in that slightly horrid expression – in the first bloom of youth. She is lovely. She is, then, so very different from Anne, who has been described as having lost her bloom. Louisa's accident produces a range of reactions. Wentworth initially 'knelt with her in his arms, looking on her with a face as pallid as her own, in an agony of silence' before his despairing cry. Mary, Anne's sister, and Henrietta, Louisa's sister, lose their heads completely. Only Anne, assisted by Captain Benwick, shows calm and good sense. She offers intelligent instruction and direction and is later counted, alongside Wentworth and Charles Musgrove, as 'completely rational'. She is a match for any man in this situation.

The visit to Lyme signals the moment when Anne's vigour begins to return. Anne – whose life has been submerged for so long – starts to rise. Her sadness begins to retreat. Her liveliness begins to bloom. Furthermore, just prior to the accident on the Cobb, Anne has drawn the attention of William Elliot, a distant cousin and heir to Kellynch Hall. Crucially, as she has been noticed by Elliot – and later becomes the subject of his pursuit – Captain Wentworth notices Elliot noticing Anne and this sparks his jealousy. If he is not yet ready to forgive Anne, he realizes that he can't bear the idea of anyone other than himself becoming attached to her.

Appearances can matter, of course. How we present ourselves in the world has consequences. If, for example, I turned up for a job interview in my pyjamas and Oodie, I should not be surprised when I'm not appointed, no matter how superb my paper qualifications. We are all bodies caught up in a world full of attitudes and mores we cannot control. We are thrown into the world. However, to be judged merely by our appearances or how we fit cultural expectations based on gender, class, sexuality, disability and so on is not holy and of God; to judge others through such prisms is wicked and sinful.

One of my favourite films is *Chariots of Fire*, the story of the British gold medal winners at the 1924 Olympics, Harold

Abrahams and Eric Liddell. Liddell is a Christian and an evangelist as well as an athlete. He has this line, which, despite the film's wild differences from *Persuasion*, resonates here: 'Where does the strength to run the race come from? Within.' Anne has had a dreadful time since her break with Wentworth. She has sunk down within herself, yet in the depths she has found clarity, reasonableness and the sheer determination to carry on. She has acquired character. She is able to act in the world in such a way that she can make decisions while about her others lose their heads. She is lovely and beautiful and this is not predicated on how she looks. I think she shows something about what we can be like in the hands of the living God; she shows us how we look in the delighting sight of God.

God of Passion and Resurrection, we are never so far from you that we cannot be raised to new life. May I learn to trust you and your never-failing love. Amen.

Day 38

'I regard Louisa Musgrove as a very amiable, sweet-tempered girl, and not deficient in understanding, but Benwick is something more. He is a clever man, a reading man; and I confess, that I do consider his attaching himself to her with some surprise. Had it been the effect of gratitude, had he learnt to love her, because he believed her to be preferring him, it would have been another thing. But I have no reason to suppose it so. It seems, on the contrary, to have been a perfectly spontaneous, untaught feeling on his side, and this surprises me. A man like him, in his situation! with a heart pierced, wounded, almost broken! Fanny Harville was a very superior creature, and his attachment to her was indeed attachment. A man does not recover from such a devotion of the heart to such a woman. He ought not; he does not.'

Either from the consciousness, however, that his friend had recovered, or from other consciousness, he went no farther; and Anne who, in spite of the agitated voice in which the latter part had been uttered, and in spite of all the various noises of the room, the almost ceaseless slam of the door, and ceaseless buzz of persons walking through, had distinguished every word, was struck, gratified, confused, and beginning to breathe very quick, and feel an hundred things in a moment. (*Persuasion*, chapter 20)

In fashionable Bath, Captain Wentworth and Anne renew their acquaintance. Wentworth has witnessed William Elliot trying to court Anne and it has piqued his jealousy. Furthermore, Anne and he have also received news that Louisa Musgrove is to marry Captain Benwick. This engagement developed in the wake of Louisa's fall at Lyme Regis, as she recovered in the home of the Harvilles. Benwick regularly reads to her and in the midst of his deep grief over the death of his betrothed, Fanny, Captain Harville's sister, they become attached. Not least among the reasons why Wentworth is surprised about the attachment is the depth of feeling he supposed Benwick to hold for Fanny; equally, he cannot quite believe that the bookish Benwick is a good match for the lively Louisa.

Of course, our attention is drawn to Wentworth's statement about devotion: 'A man does not recover from such a devotion of the heart to such a woman. He ought not; he does not.' Ostensibly it is a reference to Benwick's love for Fanny Harville. We hear, and Anne hears it, differently: as gesturing towards Wentworth's (presumed *former*) passion for her. Suddenly, we are on explosive emotional ground. Wentworth knows it; Anne knows it. Despite all the noise and background action, the ceaseless buzz, we enter intimate time and space. Anne hears Wentworth alluding to his now-distant but still life-changing passion for her; Wentworth's voice shakes as he half-consciously speaks his truth out loud. In this intimate moment, Anne's perspective fills the space. Wentworth and Anne have travelled far from one another over the previous eight and a half years, but in one sentence they are forced to re-engage with the facts of their emotional history. The sub-text is so foregrounded it might as well be hyper-text.

It is the word 'recover' which holds my attention. It holds implications of 'come back' and 'return' as well as 'regain health'. It can mean 'procure' and 'acquire again'. Wentworth suggests that any man who has experienced the deep work of the heart – as Benwick and he have – should not be able to 'come back' from the devotion he felt for his beloved. He should not be able to regain his health – his wholeness, his pristine unsullied soul, his capacity for the spontaneous overflow of love. He suggests that when someone has encountered certain kinds of loves, and certain sorts of grief, they cannot procure again the flex and stretch in their heart for new love. There is, Wentworth implies, a tragedy at the end of lost love and the death of its promise. We go on, but we are permanently changed by the loss.

Well, perhaps I overplay the point. Perhaps I make this sound more capital R 'romantic' than the novel permits. However, I do think there is force in this reading. When we have been in the hands of another and have exposed our whole life, our heart to them, and that person is – for whatever reason – no longer there, there is huge cost. The death of a loved one is a soul event, no matter how expected. The soul undergoes a kind of education in the limits of mortal life. I've also known the death of a relationship that I imagined would last a lifetime. It did not. When my then partner ended the relationship, I grieved for years. I have learned to love again, but not quite in the manner I could when young. Human beings have hearts that break and our hope and promise grow back through the scars.

Wentworth talks of 'ought'. A bishop once said to me, in regard to my ministry, beware of the 'hardening of the oughteries', suggesting one should be wary of seemingly ethical obligations that are driven more by guilt than love. In matters of the heart and soul, I am inclined to stay with 'is' rather than the 'ought'. I have come to believe that to live well is to live with a certain kind of openness to a world and to relationships which cannot be made safe from loss. I think this because I believe this is the way of Christ. We are not called to walk the exact same path as Jesus. His work, which is the work of salvation, is not ours. Still, we are called to take up the cross and follow him. This is not a path of comfort and ease. I do not think anyone should seek out loss and suffering, but to live in the sweet spot of love's mysteries means being exposed enough to others and the world that our hearts might be broken. And in that exposure, we shall not all stay the same, but we might be saved.

Loving God, may I be unafraid this day to stay close to you. May I find my safety in your lavish grace. Help me to love my neighbour as myself. Amen.

Day 39

'No, no, it is not man's nature. I will not allow it to be more man's nature than woman's to be inconstant and forget those they do love, or have loved. I believe the reverse. I believe in a true analogy between our bodily frames and our mental; and that as our bodies are the strongest, so are our feelings; capable of bearing most rough usage, and riding out the heaviest weather.'

'Your feelings may be the strongest,' replied Anne, 'but the same spirit of analogy will authorise me to assert that ours are the most tender. Man is more robust than woman, but he is not longer lived; which exactly explains my view of the nature of their attachments. Nay, it would be too hard upon you, if it were otherwise. You have difficulties, and privations, and dangers enough to struggle with. You are always labouring and toiling, exposed to every risk and hardship. Your home, country, friends, all quitted. Neither time, nor health, nor life, to be called your own. It would be hard, indeed' (with a faltering voice), 'if woman's feelings were to be added to all this.'

'We shall never agree upon this question,' Captain Harville was beginning to say, when a slight noise called their attention to Captain Wentworth's hitherto perfectly quiet division of the room. It was nothing more than that his pen had fallen down; but Anne was startled at finding him nearer than she had supposed, and half inclined to suspect that the pen had only fallen because he had been occupied by them, striving to catch sounds, which yet she did not think he could have caught.

'Have you finished your letter?' said Captain Harville.

'Not quite, a few lines more. I shall have done in five minutes.'

'There is no hurry on my side. I am only ready whenever you are. I am in very good anchorage here,' (smiling at Anne,) 'well supplied, and want for nothing. No hurry for a signal at all. Well, Miss Elliot,' (lowering his voice,) 'as I was saying we shall never agree, I suppose, upon this point. No man and woman would, probably. But let me observe that all histories are against you—all stories, prose and verse. If I had such a memory as Benwick, I could bring you fifty quotations in a moment on my side the argument, and I do not think I ever opened a book in my life which had not something to say upon woman's inconstancy. Songs and proverbs, all talk of woman's fickleness. But perhaps you will say, these were all written by men.' (*Persuasion*, chapter 23)

Given that Austen's novels seemingly revolve around romantic relationships between the sexes, it is hardly surprising that her writing reflects on prevailing gender roles and the relative virtues of men and women. Today's excerpt unfolds at one of the hinge moments in *Persuasion*. When they meet in a Bath hotel, Anne Elliot and Captain Harville, Wentworth's old friend, discuss the relative constancy and merits of men and women. As they speak, Captain Wentworth listens in. Harville argues for women's inconstancy in love and affection; Anne insists otherwise. Wentworth is so moved by Anne's insistence that women will not give up on love, even when all hope is lost, that he writes her a note declaring his feelings for her. Outside the hotel, Anne and Wentworth reconcile and renew their engagement.

The relative merits of women's and men's constancy and consistency can appear rather old-fashioned. In our own era, in which women's position in society has shifted so much, the notion that women should be seen as flaky, inconstant and ruled by changing emotions can seem absurd. We no longer live in an age in which claims that women are driven by 'wandering wombs' and attendant 'hysteria' will stick. Nonetheless, as toxic and heated culture war 'debates' about what constitutes a woman (and, by implication, a man) have metastasized, it is clear that gender essentialism is curiously persistent. If those debates are less about constancy of emotion and more about biological bits, to my surprise there are still so many who need to believe that men are (like) *this* and women are (like) *that* ... Sexed bodies are so often still seen as determining destinies.

Part of Anne's surety about the constancy of her affections is drawn from her mature and considered self-understanding. She simply knows that, despite everything, her affections for Wentworth haven't changed. She is clear that generalizations about her sex simply will not do. Her love for Wentworth is not drawn from the 'off-the-shelf' stereotypes of romantic fiction. Part of the reason that Anne Elliot is such a satisfying character is that she speaks out of the experience of a grown woman who truly knows her mind and has an educated heart. In patriarchal terms, she may have lost her 'youthful bloom'. She is much more: a person of depth, not to be read merely in terms of conventions of beauty and surface good looks.

Nonetheless, like so many women still, she negotiates a narrative which is biased against her. Harville's line regarding the long history and records concerning women's inconstancy – 'perhaps you will say, these were all written by men' – is witty and playful, of course; it also mainlines into the consistent experience of women from a wide spectrum of backgrounds and experiences. Women have so rarely been permitted to write their own stories and lives, and even when they have, they have been writing into an undertow of patriarchal assumptions and presumptions. I am reminded of 'Diving Into the Wreck', the poem by the late, great US poet Adrienne Rich, in which she explores the metaphor of women as deep-sea divers searching the wrecks of history for their own stories and finding only absence. Jane Austen was no feminist in the modern sense, but she articulated middle-class women's lives on fresh terms. Anne Elliot has a quiet, insistent and resilient determination not to be read through Harville's lens.

Constancy and determination, and a faithfulness to the requirements of a love that persists, are perhaps a little old-fashioned. Oh, well. Perhaps one of the comforts and countercultural challenges of the Christian faith is a preparedness to inhabit some things which appear old-fashioned. Certainly, I think Lent presents an opportunity to consider again the demands of constancy and determination. As some of the gospel's main characters demonstrate, not least Simon Peter and indeed most of Jesus' male disciples, it is not necessarily shameful to be inconstant. So many of the apostles have a genius for running away, for betrayal and for doubt. It is, of course, primarily the women of the Gospels who stay with Jesus. Indeed, there is a folk story that claims that the reason we have the account of Jesus' agony in the Garden is because the women stayed awake while the men slept. Certainly, it was the Blessed Virgin Mary and other women (along with John) who stayed with Jesus in his agony on the cross; it is a woman – Mary Magdalene – who was the first witness to the Resurrection. It is faithful, constant, determined and risk-taking women who witness to both the death of Jesus and his Resurrection. They teach us to stay with the trouble and then dare to find the hope.

Waiting God, you know us better than we can ever know ourselves. Thank you for your steadfastness and forgiveness especially when we fail to live according to your love. Abide with me this day. Amen.

Day 40

'I can listen no longer in silence. I must speak to you by such means as are within my reach. You pierce my soul. I am half agony, half hope. Tell me not that I am too late, that such precious feelings are gone for ever. I offer myself to you again with a heart even more your own than when you almost broke it, eight years and a half ago. Dare not say that man forgets sooner than woman, that his love has an earlier death. I have loved none but you. Unjust I may have been, weak and resentful I have been, but never inconstant. You alone have brought me to Bath. For you alone, I think and plan. Have you not seen this? Can you fail to have understood my wishes? I had not waited even these ten days, could I have read your feelings, as I think you must have penetrated mine. I can hardly write. I am every instant hearing something which overpowers me. You sink your voice, but I can distinguish the tones of that voice when they would be lost on others. Too good, too excellent creature! You do us justice, indeed. You do believe that there is true attachment and constancy among men. Believe it to be most fervent, most undeviating, in

F. W.

I must go, uncertain of my fate; but I shall return hither, or follow your party, as soon as possible. A word, a look, will be enough to decide whether I enter your father's house this evening or never.' (*Persuasion*, chapter 23)

If Fitzwilliam Darcy's first proposal to Lizzy Bennet – for all its clumsiness and mistaken pride – is more famous, surely this letter, written by Frederick Wentworth to Anne Elliot in response to her steadfast defence of constancy in love, is one of the most passionate and extraordinary addresses in all literature. Its barely restrained passion and longing make my heart hurt. Its big concept – that of a soul being pierced – is held exquisitely within the scope of Wentworth's abiding love for Anne; Wentworth's lines have been tested by time and loss in a way that cannot be matched by the love of Lizzy and Darcy. This is a letter of a person who has known love, rejection and loss and what it means, stretched out over nearly a decade of private pain and public success. It is a wonder.

It is also the product of waiting, in which hope has never quite departed but has grown threadbare. I'm not even sure if Wentworth realizes he has been waiting all this time. I suspect he has become so inured to his situation that he has believed for many years that he is OK. However, in the light of Anne's conversation with Harville, the dam has burst. Quietly, maybe half-consciously, he has always loved Anne. His anger has provided a kind of barrier to the truth; now the anger will no longer hold back the truth. Now, he must speak:

> Tell me not that I am too late, that such precious feelings are gone for ever. I offer myself to you again with a heart even more your own than when you almost broke it, eight years and a half ago. Dare not say that man forgets sooner than woman, that his love has an earlier death. I have loved none but you.

In his extraordinary book about the cost of love, W. H. Vanstone writes, 'Where the object of love is truly an "other", the activity of love is always precarious.'[1] The long wait Wentworth and Anne experience before they come back together is a tale about the cost of love. It is an education in the wonder of otherness and the extraordinary cost of true relationship. When I think of the gift of having known the people I've loved, I become aware of how they always exceeded any conception I had of them. They always remained a mystery. We are mysteries to one another and mysteries to ourselves. Only in God

---

1 W. H. Vanstone, *Love's Endeavour, Love's Expense* (London: Darton, Longman and Todd, 2007), p. 46.

are we fully known, and we have such limited purchase on ourselves. We are creatures who live such bewildering and busy
lives that even in those moments when we glimpse a little of
ourselves, we doubt it. For as much as we might wish to take
hold of the Christian invitation to find ourselves and others
in the gift of the Living God – his Body – we remain creatures
negotiating separateness. Again, Vanstone captures the pro-
fundity and pathos that can be generated in the unavoidable
gap between different and separate bodies, selves and people,
and their desire for and call to love:

> Between the self and the other there always exists, as it were,
> a 'gap' which the aspiration of love may fail to bridge or tran-
> scend ... Herein lies the poignancy of love, and its potential
> tragedy. The activity of love contains no assurance or certain-
> ty of completion: much may be expended and little achieved.[2]

Could what we experience as love – in its various forms, from the
erotic to the filial to the sacrificial – be *love* if it were assured and
safe and secure at every point? If precariousness was redacted
out? For Vanstone, the answer is no. In Vanstone's words,
'Love proceeds by no assured programme.'[3] Indeed, there is a
profoundly improvisatory structure to love. I think 'improvise'
is the right word in this context. In Latin it has implications of
'unforeseen', of 'unstudied' and 'not prepared beforehand'. It
resists the programmatic. I am not suggesting that there is no
intentionality or structure to our loving relationships; rather,
they are not reducible to technique or system, not least because
they unfold in the realm of the human and therefore the mysterious. Loving relationship requires a sense that the other holds
mystery and agency. It exceeds our temptations to want control or predictability and vice versa. Love is adventurous and
open-textured. It is indwelling. If it is to be love, as we have

---

2 Vanstone, *Love's Endeavour*, p. 46.
3 Vanstone, *Love's Endeavour*, p. 46.

seen, it cannot be coercive or forced. It has to have openness, the possibility of tragedy and the stature of waiting.

Whether we are naturally affectionate or not, I do think we are called to this radical openness and generosity in our relationships. It is a way of gentleness and trust that reveals the character of God. It is passionate but not insistent. It is also something we are invited to show towards ourselves as we seek to get to know God and ourselves better. Love is costly, but it is our vocation. As we prepare to leave Lent and turn towards the passion and resurrection of our Lord I want, and I hope you want, to centre on that costly love and ask: how can I, how can we, step as seriously, hopefully and determinedly towards the cross of love and the Day of Resurrection as we dare.

Generous God, help me to greet you with gladness and trust this day. Grant me faith and hope and, most of all, love. Amen.

Postscript

'I cannot fix on the hour, or the spot, or the look, or the words, which laid the foundation. It is too long ago. I was in the middle before I knew that I had begun.'

At the close of *Pride and Prejudice*, Lizzy asks Darcy when he had begun to love her. His answer is captured above. If you've stayed with this book for the 40 days of Lent and you were a relative newbie to the world of Austen, I trust you now know that she is about much more than *Pride and Prejudice*. Nonetheless, these words of Darcy struck me as a good place to begin this postscript.

'I was in the middle before I knew I had begun.' Darcy may be speaking about his love for one other person, Lizzy Bennet, but he speaks powerfully into my faith and the ebbs and flows of my half-understood, often bewildered life. As I've sought to make sense of God and who he is calling me to be, I've found myself again and again forced to recognize that I feel thrown into the world; that life, even the most flourishing life, is lived *in media res*. The more time I've spent with God, the more comfortable I've become with that sense of irresolution and complexity. Why tell you this here? Well, simply to remind you that no matter how holy or how focused or amazing your Lent has been, there is no such thing as closure or completion, not in this life. Yes, we are about to enter into the wonder of the Triduum and the absolute joy of Easter, which reveal to us the love and faithfulness and reconciliation of God in wondrous ways. However, we are not – as humans – 'achievements'. We do not arrive, except perhaps to begin again.

What I hope this Lenten pilgrimage with Jane Austen has revealed, however, is the primacy of love. Love – the abiding, outrageous, challenging love of God – is not to be gainsaid or short-circuited; it is not cheap or easy; it is – even in its seemingly most commonplace form – demanding. It asks of us indwelling and serious, unreserved relationship. Love – as that which is God and which is offered by God – is no slushy feeling, but that which will change the world for goodness and justice and mercy. It scares the hell out of us, so much so that we want to crucify it when it draws close. It turns the world upside down. It is always ahead of us and in the midst of us. It is the foundation and the structure; it is alive and it is life. We cannot fix it down. God will not stay still and be our faithful puppy. Love is not restricted by time and it is in all time and it is time and space in which to dwell in the truth. Love is there in the middle of us before we even knew it had begun.

As we prepare to enter into the joys of Easter, we do not abandon Lent, as if it were a phase of life to be discarded. The preparations and fasting of Lent reach forward into the joy of resurrection. We have been changed by our walk with God and perhaps we are a little better prepared to greet him on the cross and on Easter Day. I hope and pray that Jane Austen and my often inadequately expressed and quotidian remarks on her genius have enabled that deeper walk in fresh and unexpected ways. I hope you've been surprised as well as encouraged. At the very least, I trust that this Lent has not been grim, but rather an invitation into a place where delight, hope, love and promise meet. As Austen herself says, in *Mansfield Park*, so often 'Life seems but a quick succession of busy nothings.' However, when we are caught up in the rough and tumble of life's bewildering shifts and strangeness, we might also remember some other words she wrote in *Northanger Abbey*. They were spoken by the not always consistent or trustworthy Isabella. However, perhaps they could be words of Jesus himself, the one whom we can trust in his abiding love and faithfulness: 'There is nothing I would not do for those who are really my friends. I have no notion of loving people by halves, it is not my nature.' When we love fully and extravagantly, we shall meet God and be changed from glory into glory. We shall know that we too are loved beyond compare and, yet more, we are liked. We may find that in this liberation into love we shall be emboldened to live lives shaped by hope, that our sufferings are held and known and that we may taste salvation and be lifted up into New Day in our very bones.

Selected Bibliography

The novels of Jane Austen

I have worked, primarily, with the recent Penguin hardback edition of Austen's novels which includes careful and (modestly) scholarly, introductions and very helpful historical information and literary endnotes. You might also consider looking at Mollands.net, which is an online hub that includes the full text of Austen's completed novels. Do be aware that the text of the novels has slight variations from the text of the Penguin versions, both in terms of US spelling as well as slight variations in punctuation generated by the use of alternative manuscript sources.

Some secondary texts

Paula Byrne, *The Real Jane Austen: A Life in Small Things* (London: William Collins, 2013).

Paula Hollingsworth, *The Spirituality of Jane Austen* (Oxford: Lion, 2017).

Helena Kelly, *Jane Austen: The Secret Radical* (London: Icon, 2017).

Janet Todd (ed.), *Jane Austen in Context* (Cambridge: Cambridge University Press, 2005).

Lucy Worsley, *Jane Austen at Home* (London: Hodder, 2018).